Something Special

DEDICATION

Miss Renee Biggs, age sixteen, died on the evening of August ninth, Nineteen Hundred and Seventy-Seven. She was the granddaughter of Mrs. Alma D. Biggs, whose writings appear in, both, **What Are We Doing Here** and **Something Special.**

Renee was a beautiful and vibrant young lady who loved life. She was as a refreshing spring flower, giving love and beauty to all who knew her. It is to the lovely memory of Renee Biggs that we dedicate the cover and contents of this book.

Peggy Simpson

Something Special

Associated Women's Organization

Mars Hill Bible School

QUALITY PUBLICATIONS

P.O. BOX 1060   ABILENE, TEXAS 79604

Any profit from the sales of the book will go to the:

Associated Women's Organization
Mars Hill Bible School
698 Cox Creek Parkway
Florence, Alabama 35630

1st Printing—May, 1977
2nd Printing—August, 1977
3rd Printing—November, 1977

ISBN: 0-89137-408-6

COMPILER'S NOTE

From looking over the chapter headings, we hope that you can recognize that there really is "Something Special" about this book. It contains some laughter and some tears, for it takes both to make a complete woman. It contains some of the innermost thoughts and dreams of twelve people but expresses the minds and hearts of hundreds.

We need to open our "heart doors" a little wider to make room for ever so many more who need loving. We could give out much more light and still have plenty to spare. Hearts that are bright and warm are like royal fireplaces inviting those who are shivering from the cold.

It is my prayer that this book will be a royal fireplace to you, making you and those around you more special.

Mrs. John P. (Peggy) Simpson
406 W. North Commons
Tuscumbia, Alabama 35674

CONTENTS

COMPILER .... Mrs. Peggy Simpson

EDITOR .... Mrs. Linda Stanley

PROOF READER .... Mrs. George Barnett

COVER DESIGN .... Miss Nanette Robbins

WHAT IS PEACE?

When Paul made peace with God, he then made war on everything that was godless. He feared nothing save the displeasure of his Lord and Master. His trials were enormous, but he had built his house upon the Rock; he had complete faith in the wisdom and love of Christ. Once when he was caught in a storm on a ship (Acts 27:22-25) and the ship's timbers were cracking, the sails ripping, the winds howling and even the salty sea-dog sailors were ready to abandon the ship, Paul stood up and stated, "And now I exhort you to be of good cheer: for there shall be no loss of any man's life among you, but of the ship . . . . Wherefore, sirs, be of good cheer: for I believe God, that it shall be even as it was told me."

That's peace in the time of storm!

In the book of Daniel we read the story of Shadrack, Meshack and Abednego. It was turn or burn for them when they refused to worship Nebuchadnezzar's gods. Listen to their answer to the king: "Oh Nebuchadnezzar, we are not careful to answer thee in this matter. If it be so, our God whom we serve is able to deliver us from the burning fiery furnace, and he will deliver us out of thine hand, O king" (Daniel 3:16-17). By the quiet, calm way in which they answered the king, their confidence in God was evident. They weren't so much concerned with *would* God rescue them, but they were sure He could do it if He chose.

That's peace in the time of storm!

1

Now, what relation is there between Shadrack, Meshack and Abednego and the apostle Paul? *Peace*—peace in the time of storm!

What is peace? The Greek authors said, "That state of affairs when there is no war." But to the Hebrew way of thinking the word peace (shalom) meant more than the mere absence of war. It carried with it the idea of having whatever would make for one's highest good. Today we hear the word used to describe all kinds of things. For example, someone may say they are searching for "peace of mind." Then you may hear a sailor speaking about a "peaceful harbour" or someone from town looking for a "peaceful place" out in the country. We often hear a mother longing for "a little peace and quiet around the house."

And so, when we begin to answer the question, "What is peace?" we find it is almost like trying to answer the question, "What is light?" We know what it is, but when we try to define it for someone else we both end up in the dark.

When we turn to the Bible we find that, like a lot of other subjects, the Bible does not define peace either. Rather than a definition, it shows us the cause of peace and the consequences of it. We also learn that peace itself is a consequence—a by-product of certain conditions and actions. This means that a search for peace as an end in itself won't work. It is the by-product of a higher search.

A teacher once asked her third-graders a very sobering question. "What," she asked, "do you think would help most to bring about peace in the world?" There were, of course, many different answers as those young minds went to work on this age-old problem. One said, "Share your toys." Another thought, "Don't talk back." Still another said, "Don't holler at anyone." One thought it would help to ban the sale of guns. But one young pupil wrote this answer: "I would tell others about Jesus." You know, it is strange to me that whenever I repeat this student's answer most people smile. I don't know why, but I do know one thing—that tender, young mind was nearer to the solution than most of the world leaders. The Master will change men, and men must change before peace is known. We will never know what true peace is apart from the Prince of Peace. However, it seems that we try to find it every other way except His way.

Consider His words recorded in John 14:27:

Peace I leave with you, my peace I give unto you: not as the world giveth, give I unto you. Let not your heart be troubled, neither let it be afraid.

What is this peace that Christ is talking about? Is it a peace that is possible for you and me, as women, to have? Is it a peace that a young mother can know? a grandmother? a middle-aged wife? a widow? He said this peace (whatever it is) is a gift. Is it free, or are there conditions?

In the minds of many of us peace is merely the lack of struggle. However, when we look at the teachings of Jesus it is hard to get this definition of peace to fit. He taught and warned that those who followed him would have just the opposite. "In the world ye shall have tribulation" (John 16:33). Nor did he mean a peace in the worldly sense of the absence of war and strife among nations, for He said, "And ye shall hear of wars and rumours of wars" (Matthew 24:6). Further, Christ said that it was *His* peace that He was giving, indicating that it was a peace that man had not previously known or experienced. As Paul said, "And the way of peace have they not known" (Romans 3:17).

What then is it? It is spiritual peace—the peace that is the consequence of freedom from the burden and guilt of sin and a by-product of a right relationship with the God of heaven. "Therefore being justified by faith, we have peace with God through our Lord Jesus Christ" (Romans 5:1); (see also Ephesians 2:13-18).

Perhaps it would help us in our understanding if we said that this "peace with God" has two different parts, or aspects, to it.

First, it is a PEACE OF RECONCILIATION. The sinner is at enmity with God, but in becoming a Christian she lays down the weapons of rebellion to God's will and permits the blood of Christ to cover her sins which have separated her from God. "For if, when we were enemies, we were reconciled to God by the death of his Son. . ." (Romans 5:10). Thus, "He is our peace" (Ephesians 2:14). He has made peace between God and man.

Another feature of this peace of reconciliation involves our relationship with others. Isaiah had heard God say, "Peace, peace to him that is far off, and to him that is near" (Isaiah 57:19). Paul explained: "And (Christ) came and preached peace to you which were afar off (Gentiles), and to them that were nigh (Jews)'' (Ephesians 2:17). So we have another consequence of Christ's death, peace between men. "For he is our peace, who hath made both one. . .And that he might reconcile both unto God in one body by the cross, having slain the enmity thereby'' (Ephesians 2:14,16).

Thus, we have a peace of reconciliation—a reconciliation between God and man, and a reconciliation between man and man.

But that isn't all there is to this peace with God. There is a second aspect which could be called the PEACE OF CONFIDENCE, and it has to do with our relationship with God as his child. You recall that Jesus said, "My peace I give unto you" (John 15:27). The peace that He himself enjoyed has been made possible for us, which is the peace that comes from being a child of God—peace *within*. As children of God, you and I no longer have to dread and fear the Creator, for now we can come boldly unto the throne of mercy as children to our father. (See Hebrews 4:16; 10:19-22; Ephesians 3:12; I John 4:17.) Just as does Christ, we too can call Him our Father and have the same peace that Christ had from such a relationship. Let's look at some things that tell us this statement is true.

One of the greatest human needs is to feel secure. A happy child is one who knows that he is loved and that mother and father will take care of his every need. And a happy wife is one who knows that she is loved—that her relationship with her husband is secure. This is a longing in every heart, and there is nothing that fills this longing like that of being a child of God. There is no one who is more secure than a faithful child of the Lord.

Christ revealed this to us in many different ways. He said that a small sparrow cannot fall dead without attracting the attention of God, and that if God cares for something so insignificant, He certainly cares for us. To show just how well God knows us, He told us that even the number of hairs on our head is known by the Father. On another occasion he made this comparison: "If you then, who are evil, know how to give good gifts to your children, how much more will your Father who is in heaven give good things to those who ask him" (Matthew 7:11 RSV). Suppose one of your children came in one day and said, "Mother, I need help. I know that you and Dad have had much more experience than I have and that you can help me avoid a lot of trouble if I will listen to you. And I really do want to be happy and to make you and Dad happy. If you will guide me and help me, I'll do my very best to follow your advice.'' What would you do? (Besides faint!) Would you turn around and try to do everything you could to make her life miserable, confused and unhappy? What parent would?

Now, here's a child of God who has come to the Father in prayer asking Him to guide her life and help her to be a child in whom He can be well pleased. Will the Father then set out to foul that person's life up? What did Christ say? If you as a parent here on earth are concerned with the security of your children and are willing to do all you can to help them and guide them and make their life a happy one, then HOW MUCH MORE will your Father who is in heaven give good things to you!

What does this have to do with peace? Well, it goes back to that great human need to feel secure. Just as a child who realizes that her parents love her and will care for and protect her with all their power is a peaceful child—so also is the relationship enjoyed by the child of God. Part of the peace that Christ made possible for us is the security of a relationship.

Finally, a peaceful soul is a trusting soul. In Matthew 8 we read about Christ and the disciples being caught out in a boat during a storm. The boat was being tossed about by the waves and the wind, and the disciples were becoming more anxious and upset by the minute. They looked at Jesus and found that He was asleep. Unable to stand their mounting fear, they cried out for Him to save them. "And he saith unto them, 'Why are ye fearful, O ye of little faith?' Then he arose, and rebuked the winds and the sea; and there was a great calm" (Matthew 8:26). The question comes: "How could they have been so frightened with Christ in the boat?" The same question comes back: "How can we?" Did not the same Jesus say to all of us, "And, lo, I am with you always, even unto the end of the world" (Matthew 28:20).

Whenever I read about His calming the storm, I remember the time our son caught a bird that he was going to "tame." I can still see how, when he held it in his hands, the wild look of fright showed in its eyes and its little heart throbbed against his fingers. He couldn't make it at peace by merely holding his hands still. He had to teach the little bird to trust him. But finally, after many days of patience and care, it gained confidence. Its wild look was gone, and it would rest peacefully in our son's small hands. And so it is with you and me—the greater our trust in God, the greater our peace of mind. This is why the apostle Paul could say, "Be careful (or anxious) for nothing; but in every thing by prayer and supplication with thanksgiving let your requests be made known unto God. And the peace of God, which passeth all understanding, shall keep your hearts and minds through Christ Jesus" (Philippians 4:6-7). A peaceful soul is a trusting soul.

Peace is knowing that:

All things work together for good to them that love God, to them who are the called according to his purpose (Romans 8:28).

Neither death, nor life, nor angels, nor principalities, nor powers, nor things present, nor things to come, nor height, nor depth, nor any other creature, shall be able to separate us from the love of God, which is in Christ Jesus our Lord (Romans 8:38-39).

There is therefore now no condemnation to them which are in Christ Jesus. . .(Romans 8:1).

There hath no temptation taken you but such as is common to man: but God is faithful, who will not suffer you to be tempted above that ye are able; but will with the temptation also make a way to escape, that ye may be able to bear it (I Corinthians 10:13).

Blessed is the man that endureth temptation: for when he is tried, he shall receive the crown of life, which the Lord hath promised to them that love him (James 1:12).

And this is the promise that he hath promised us, even eternal life (I John 2:25).

And being fully persuaded that, what he had promised, he was also able to perform (Romans 4:21).

. . .he that endureth to the end shall be saved (Matthew 10:22).

To an inheritance incorruptible, and undefiled, and that fadeth not away, reserved in heaven for you (I Peter 1:4).

Let not your heart be troubled: ye believe in God, believe also in me. In my Father's house are many mansions: if it were not so, I would have told you. I go to prepare a place for you. And if I go and prepare a place for you, I will come again, and receive you unto myself; that where I am, there ye may be also (John 14:1-3).

What is peace? "Come unto me, all ye that labour and are heavy laden, and I will give you rest. Take my yoke upon you, and learn of me; for I am meek and lowly in heart: and *ye shall find rest unto your souls*" (Matthew 11:28-29).

Rest for the soul; that is peace. Only the Prince of Peace would give such an invitation—only the Prince of Peace could.

Mrs. Valera McGuire
Route 4
Muscle Shoals City, Alabama

LEARNING TO MEET
A
CHALLENGE

Introduction

When asked to have a part in this book I was extremely touched. The topic given to me is a very exciting one. I feel as though the Christian life is one continuous challenge. The way Christian women handle life's challenges is important to everyone with whom they come in contact, whether it be husband, children, parents, fellow-Christians or the world. Well-met challenges might be considered stepping stones to heaven.

The world is watching our actions and reactions as Christian women; therefore, we must meet the challenge for God our Maker, and Jesus Christ our Saviour. Do we really take a stand for the truth when we are confronted with moral or scriptural issues? How do we handle these? Are we weak, and do we act as the heathen that had no God? Let's meet the challenges that face us as Christian women—even this very day.

Three types of challenges will be discussed in this chapter:
1. Meeting the challenge as a Christian woman.
2. Meeting the challenge as a Christian wife.
3. Meeting the challenge as a Christian mother.

Meeting the Challenge as a Christian Woman

"The Lord is my shepherd; I shall not want" (Psalm 23:1).

In the fold of Christianity we find peace and safety when Jesus is our leader. Through Christ our Saviour and King we have complete assurance

9

that He will lead us if we will only follow. Some sheep follow their shepherd closely, some afar off, and some cease to follow at all and become lost.

Almost twenty years ago I became a part of the flock of Jesus. I was sixteen years old but very immature both physically and spiritually. As a young Christian I did not begin to understand the responsibilities that accompany the Christian life. I was one of His sheep and He was my shepherd; but I followed afar off—only a babe in Christ but still a part of the great Church for whom Jesus died. After marriage and more study of God's Word, I began to realize the awesome challenge of being a Christian example. I can't change the mistakes already made; but I can use every opportunity through the wisdom and teachings of the Bible to influence others for Christ, especially the youth of today.

No one is half as interested in what we say as in what we do. We can challenge others not with advice so much as with actions. Many times just a smile, a gentle touch, a tender word or a small act of kindness will exemplify a Christ-like attitude. As Christian women let's meet the challenge of example by the demonstration of love and service to our God by serving our fellowman.

"Your adversary the devil, as a roaring lion, walketh about seeking whom he may devour" (I Peter 5:8).

Today America is faced with a mass of wickedness: dope, free-love or pre-marital sex, liquor, extremely immodest dress and nudity, abortion, the acceptance of homosexuality as a way of life, obscene literature available to almost any age. But the most dangerous evil facing us could be atheistic evolution and the lack of Biblical knowledge to combat it. Communism is on the rise because we have failed to take a stand against its ungodly principles. One day we may wake up and find ourselves in a similar position as the Jews who were carried away to Babylon.

In the Old Testament we read that God's chosen people were perishing for lack of knowledge. Today elders and preachers are pleading for back to the Bible study. Just as our physical bodies need nutritious foods to function properly, our spiritual life must have an ample supply of spiritual food. The study of God's word is a challenge that can be the most rewarding and pleasure-filled part of your day. Many problems can be solved through the great wisdom of His word. Communication plays a vital part in our relationship with God. Do not neglect to rely on God for spiritual strength through the wonderful blessing and privilege of prayer. Our Lord and Master Teacher taught His disciples to pray, and as saints in the Kingdom of God we are to pattern ourselves after His example. Prayer and Bible study will change worries, frustrations and anxieties into a deeper trusting faith in our God and develop peace and happiness in this life. You can meet this challenge. Plan a devotional period as part of your day.

Christian women (girls) are also challenged today in matters of dress. Today's fashions include backless, bottomless, braless, thighless and stomachless clothing. Christians should not be tempted to wear these; instead, they should use every opportunity to teach others through love and compassion the consequences of immodest clothing.

The story of David and Bathsheba illustrates how one can be led away from God by the lust of the eyes. David walked out on the roof at eventide and saw a woman washing herself. The woman was very beautiful to look upon. David was said to be a man after God's own heart, but he took another man's wife and even committed murder because of this woman (2 Samuel 11:2-27).

Dressing modestly is an important challenge, but there is a more unique challenge in adorning the heart and soul with godliness as we strive to live the Christian life. God gives us instructions in 1 Timothy 2:9: "In like manner also, that women adorn themselves in modest apparel, with shamefacedness and sobriety; not with braided hair, or gold, or pearls, or costly array; but (which becometh women professing godliness) with good works."

One person in particular comes to my mind as a pattern of a godly woman. She is Mrs. Ralph (Ruby) Snell. I have known her since I was a young girl. She met the challenge of adorning herself in modest apparel and passed it on to her daughters and even to her granddaughters. Her life speaks for itself. It tells the world and everyone that knows her she is truly the pattern of a righteous woman. Her influence has been instilled into 10 children and 16 grandchildren. I was touched by her life, and I am sure there are many lives she has influenced by her modest dress and her gentle, Christ-like example.

"But the tongue can no man tame; it is an unruly evil, full of deadly poison" (James 3:8).

The challenge of an unruly tongue is probably the most difficult one for women. Many times we say things without realizing we have offended others or perhaps even encouraged gossip. Thoughtfulness might be considered the key in dealing with this problem. Being very careful to think before we speak and remembering the "Golden Rule" will help us to be successful in meeting this challenge.

Me—Act Like Jesus? This was the arresting title of a book I picked up at the bookstore one day. For weeks I couldn't get this thought out of my mind. Why do you suppose it made such a deep impression? The word ME stuck like glue in my mind as I remembered Jesus saying, "And he that taketh not his cross, and followeth after me, is not worthy of me" (Matthew 10:38). Our Lord and Saviour set the example, but we have to be willing to follow in His footsteps. Me act like Jesus? Yes—in example, attitude, dress and speech—we as members of His Church can and must do so.

Meeting the Challenge As a Christian Wife

God's infinite wisdom has set forth a unique challenge for a successful marriage. His instructions are clear:

Therefore as the church is subject unto Christ, so let the wives be to their own husbands in everything (Ephesians 5:24).

Therefore shall a man leave his father and his mother, and shall cleave unto his wife; and they shall be one flesh (Genesis 2:24).

Husbands, love your wives, even as Christ also loved the church, and gave himself for it (Ephesians 5:25).

Christian husbands and wives share love and concern for one another, but more important, they share love, worship and service to God as they strive to build a happy marriage. Many problems are solved when we learn to place God first, partner second and self third.

After 17 years of sharing an extremely happy marriage, my husband and I believe the most important ingredients (apart from placing God first) are: understanding, cooperation, determination and an unselfish love for each other. Examine your marriage as we discuss each of these challenges.

Understanding people is an art, and nowhere is this talent needed more than in marriage, especially during the first few years. To understand that God made men and women completely different is a vital aspect of a marital relationship. Sometimes women become very disturbed over the lack of emotion shown by their husbands. Most men do not openly display their concern, fear, excitement or compassion as much as do women. However, they may have many explosive emotions bottled inside. Understanding their different emotional make-up could be a sign of maturity on our part.

When you marry, do not think you can change the personality of your mate to any great extent. Learn to understand and accept him the way he is. One of the most difficult challenges for me has been to understand that my husband needs a quiet time in which to rest, dream, recreate, plan and meditate upon God and His word. Understanding and accepting each other's needs is a task that encompasses unselfishness, fairness and complete communication between each other. A couple with different educational, financial or religious backgrounds might need an extra measure of patience in meeting this challenge, but the rewards will be countless. As mutual understanding grows, love and respect for each other abound. A closeness develops so that you more fully understand the scripture, ". . .and they shall become one flesh."

Cooperation naturally should be added to understanding in achieving a successful marriage. To cooperate is simply to work or act together.

Lack of cooperation in financial matters will make it very hard to survive the stress and strains of monthly bills. A budget can be one of the best marriage counselors. To plan a budget you need to list your income and expenditures, adding a few dollars for those extras that might be unexpected. No matter how good a budget looks on paper, it will only work when we stay within its guidelines. Placing God first in your plans is really the key to success. Meeting this challenge as partners with God, desiring only to please Him, will bring the blessings He has promised.

Perhaps cooperation is the secret to a peaceful atmosphere in our homes. After 16 years of marriage I told someone that we have never had a fuss or quarrel in our home. It seemed very hard for her to believe this. We have our share of problems as in all homes, but we settle them in a peaceful manner. When problems arise, the first thing that comes to my mind is God's command that my husband is to be the head of this family. As head of our home he is our protection from pitfalls and dangers as well as our leader in both material and spiritual matters. I must trust his wisdom in the decisions he makes. Both partners must have an unselfish attitude and cooperate to have a peace-filled home. Peace in a home doesn't just happen—it has to be worked at. A cooperative environment produces a type of peace and contentment that seems to be a rare quality in marriages of today. When a problem arises in your family, here are some suggestions to help meet the challenge of being a peacemaker:

1. If the choice is between right or wrong, there should be no problem of choice.

2. Take time to think about the problem or disagreement before discussing it.

3. Sit down together and discuss the problem in a quiet and understanding manner. Give everyone a chance to express themselves.

4. Let the husband make the final decision. Male leadership is vital in the home.

5. Learn to say, "I'm sorry."

6. "Be angry, but sin not" (Psalms 4:4 RSV). Cursing, yelling, fighting or saying hateful words will make a problem larger.

7. Compromise when needed.

8. Be quick to forgive and FORGET.

9. Last, but most important, consult the Word of God for wisdom and strength.

Perhaps the majority of problems with in-laws are caused by the lack of cooperation. Many times wives have a tendency to be jealous and selfish. I have been blessed with wonderful in-laws, and I am thankful to God for their love and concern for me. Let me share an idea that has played an important part in building our good relationship. From the beginning of our marriage, my husband and I have not criticized each other's parents. Faultfinding and knit-picking are dangerous traps we avoided. Being kind, gentle and thoughtful to his parents will encourage him to love and appreciate you more. Remember, the best sons make the best husbands.

Although a marriage could not survive on this ingredient alone, *determination* definitely plays a part in a successful marriage. Of the four ingredients listed earlier, determination has been the least needed in my own marriage. Perhaps understanding and cooperation have replaced the need for determination to some extent. However, many have met and conquered the problems and challenges of marriage through sheer determination. Many a floundering marriage has survived because two people were determined to make their marriage work.

Love is the most wonderful God-given emotion. It is an unexplainable feeling we share with others. The greatest example of love is God's love in sending His only son Jesus to die for the sins of the world. A powerful love was exemplified by Jesus Christ in his willingness to suffer and die for us. With these two supreme examples I have tried to describe love's characteristics.

Love is willing.	Love shares hopes.
Love is gentle.	Love shares dreams.
Love is sharing.	Love shares sickness.
Love is giving.	Love shares burdens.
Love is protecting.	Love shares fears.
Love is unselfish.	Love shares defeats.
Love is understanding.	Love shares victory.
Love is compromising.	Love shares unhappiness.
Love is forgiving.	Love shares problems.
Love is happy.	Love shares love.

In a good marriage the words, "I love you," are often heard in the home. Strive to develop an unselfish love in your marriage and challenge yourself to instill as many of the above qualities into it as possible.

As husband and wife fulfill their desires in a sexual relationship, they are expressing love for each other. Physical love is a vital part of marriage and brings contentment and fulfillment when engaged in as God has planned. This relationship is personal, not to be joked about or made light of but to be considered sacred and beautiful.

Over the years as a marriage unfolds into a masterpiece, it seems understanding, cooperation and determination are just by-products of the main ingredient—LOVE.

Meeting the Challenge as a Christian Mother

God, help us to give our children good roots. The sturdiest, most productive plants are those that have a solid base and go deep into the soil. Our Christian homes might be compared to a garden with rich soil. A family needs soil enriched with good talk, good music, good books and good taste. But above all let it have goodness of spirit and goodness in our actions toward one another. Let's be sure we fertilize with the Word of God.

In supplying our children with good roots we encounter many challenges. Our children need love, discipline, understanding, praise and most of all they need to be taught to love and respect God and His word. To develop these characteristics into the lives of our children we must first set an example. As our children look to us for wisdom and guidance they desperately need to see the pattern of a godly life before them. So many of our young people are in search of adult leadership. An examination of our examples will often aid us in meeting this challenge.

Proper discipline demonstrates love and instills security in the lives of our children. "The rod and reproof give wisdom: but a child left to himself bringeth his mother to shame" (Proverbs 29:15). Discipline should begin at birth. Even a little one needs to know who is in authority. A well-known pediatrician in our area gave some new parents an interesting bit of information. He said, "This baby came to live with you, you didn't go to live with it." It was necessary for this baby to adjust to the life style of the parents.

Both parents need to agree on the type of discipline in the home. Disagreements are found in every home. As parents we need to discuss these in private in order to stand united in front of our children. Some children will watch to see if one parent is on his side and then will play one parent against the other. This problem might produce an unstable atmosphere in our homes if allowed to become a pattern.

Discipline must be consistent. I have heard young people say, "Boy, when my mom feels good I can get away with anything; but when she feels bad, the least thing I do, I get it!" I shall never forget watching a lady and her child one day. She told the child over and over not to do a certain thing. Each time she spoke she said, "If you do that again I am going to spank you." The child continued to disobey, but that spanking never came. Consistency requires discipline on the part of parents. Our son told me when he was in the 6th grade (now 12th grade) that he always knew what to expect from his daddy. Even as a very young lad his daddy thought consistency was extremely important to their relationship. We have made mistakes and will make many more in the next few years, but I do feel consistent discipline has been a valuable asset in dealing with our problems.

Compassion, a prayerful attitude and concern for the child's welfare are vital qualities when administering correction. When these qualities are apparent, your children know you are going to be fair with your discipline. When they sense fairness, they will in turn develop the proper attitude toward accepting correction.

Listen to the wisdom of God concerning discipline in Proverbs 29:17: "Correct thy son, and he shall give thee rest; yea, he shall give delight unto thy soul." Many parents lie down at night and that uncorrected son or daughter hangs heavy on their thoughts, and there is no rest. The second part of this verse tells us that well-disciplined children will make us happy. We have all known young people who were well-mannered and delightful to be around. This type of behavior doesn't just happen—someone is responsible.

While working with children and teenagers at school and teenage girls in Bible classes, I have learned many valuable lessons. Right at the top of the list I would put the importance of respect. They will respect you if you demand their respect. Once you have their respect, they will obey your rules and, amazingly, will like you for demanding that they do. As we demand respect and obedience from our youth we are preparing their minds to render respect and obedience to God.

Plenty of sunlight is a must for healthy plants. God's word is the sunlight in the lives of our children. We must see that they get a sufficient supply of Biblical knowledge to protect them from the influence of Satan. Many times we become upset and overly anxious when our children fail to accomplish those things required of them in school. And rightly so. We should be concerned. But how much more important is the need to teach our children the inspired Word of God. The child's spiritual development is primarily the responsibility of the home; the Sunday school exists to assist the home. Jewish parents taught their children at every opportunity. We live in the Christian Age and have the perfect plan of salvation, but we seem to be failing to instill in our children the desire to live for God. Jot down the number of hours spent watching television compared with hours spent in the study of God's

Word in your home. Parents who enjoy meditating upon the Word of God will instill the desire for spiritual food in their children by example.

An ample supply of rainfall is necessary for root development in the plant kingdom. For our children to develop deep roots spiritually they need a sufficient supply of prayer in their lives. Pray that your children will love God and develop a trusting faith in Him. From the time they are small, pray for their marriage to Christians. Let them hear you pray for these things and teach them the reasons for doing so. Have lessons on prayer in your home so they will understand the greatness of talking to our God. Nourish their lives daily with prayer to develop an attitude of dependence upon God. As they mature they will draw strength and courage from prayer to aid them in times of trial and temptation.

Roots are cultivated with tools. An important tool needed by Christian parents in rearing their children is time. For their roots to be strong we must spend time loving, training and teaching our young people. There must be a time to talk, a time to listen, a time to be a friend, a time to share, a time for God. Setting aside time for your children is not an easy task in the busy world in which we live. Mothers with daughters have a frightening responsibility in educating and guiding them in the ways of righteousness. Many hours must be involved if communication, trust and confidence are to surround your relationship. Meet this challenge and supply the time needed to give your children good roots.

Finally, Paul reminds us of the ultimate challenge for a Christian in Philippians 3:13-14: ". . .forgetting what lies behind and straining forward to what lies ahead, I press on toward the goal for the prize of the upward call of God in Christ Jesus." May God's richest blessings be upon us as we strive to meet the challenges that confront us as His children.

Mrs. Connie Rhoden
1601 Southern Blvd.
Sheffield, Alabama

RESTORATION—
HOUSES, WOMEN, SOULS

As the years fly by we seem to realize more and more that times have changed and our traditional values are no longer held dear. Whether we admit it or not, we are caught up in a whirling, artificial stream which is the result of an affluent society. We of the 20th century are in a state of restless groping. Today, as in the long ago, it would greatly benefit all of us to heed the words of Psalms 46:10, "Be still, and know that I am God."

Now is the time to encourage the creation and preservation of a genuine appreciation of our great heritage. We all owe a debt of gratitude to our forefathers, whether we consider it great or small. "I have taught you the way of wisdom; I have led you in the paths of uprightness" (Proverbs 4:11 RSV). We can either let go or hold fast to these paths. Please join me in the preservation of all things worthy to be held dear.

Let's Restore!

Houses

Restore, I pray you, to them, even this day, their lands, their vineyards, their oliveyards, and THEIR HOUSES, also the hundredth part of the money, and of the corn, the wine, and the oil, that ye exact of them. Then said they 'We will restore them" (Nehemiah 5:11, 12a).

Through wisdom is a house builded; and by understanding it is established: and by knowledge shall the chambers be filled with all precious and pleasant riches (Proverbs 24:3-4).

The people had a mind to work (Nehemiah 4:6).

19

A great trend is noticeable these days in young and old alike—the search for nostalgia. It is the frantic seeking after mellowed things. Much importance is placed upon the piecing together of family records, finding and holding to bits of glass, books and furniture, reviving old songs, and generally cultivating an appreciation of things which tend to link us with the past. These searches seem eventually to merge into a feeling of love and appreciation of our basic heritage.

Sometimes while looking for the old way of doing things we stumble upon the old places where these things were actually practiced. Old houses seem to reflect the personality and character of the people who have called them "home." It is possible to turn the pages back in one's mind and picture the love, harmony and Christian living that went into making any old house a real home. In driving along our country roads I have many times been fascinated with the remnants of a once-charming old place far upon a hillside, seemingly waiting for someone to offer a word of encouragement in its struggle for survival. Sometimes these calls seem so loud and clear that they are actually heard; then after much weighing of matters the task of RESTORATION is begun.

Webster defines restoration as "the act of returning to the original state." I have come to think of the word as being synonymous with the accomplishments made at the site of the T. B. Larimore Home on the campus of Mars Hill Bible School, Florence, Alabama. For our Christian heritage the Larimore Home, built in 1870, has a unique distinction and significance all its own. The sturdy walls of this building echo with the voice of our religious faith; its loving arms enfolded the hopes and dreams and longings of noble spirits who were seeking to restore New Testament Christianity.

The beautiful seasons, each crowned with its particular charm, have made a panorama of color as the parade of years marched by this spacious home framed by virgin oaks, elms, beeches and hickories. No one seemed to recognize the faint sound from this knoll of nature's beauty as being a plea for extension of life.

Join me now in a bit of nostalgia as I turn the pages back approximately 103 years to the time when this stately twelve-room home was another dream, and picture it in its original state and usefulness.

Theophilus Brown Larimore was born July 10, 1843, in Jefferson County, Tennessee. As a young man he served as a soldier in the Civil War. In the battle of Shiloh he was assigned to watch the Tennessee River for the coming of Union gunboats. He wrote the message that informed General Albert S. Johnston, who was killed at Shiloh, of the presence on the river of two Union gunboats which were escorting a fleet of troop transports. Soon after the war the Larimore family moved to Hopkinsville, Kentucky. There the young T. B. Larimore heard the gospel, obeyed it and soon after preached his first gospel sermon.

In 1868 he came to North Alabama where he met and married a lovely young lady by the name of Esther Gresham. The ceremony was performed near the place he later named Mars Hill, which is located about four miles from downtown Florence, Alabama. Mrs. Larimore had inherited this small plot of ground from the estate of her mother. A site was selected on the summit of one of the cluster of little hills for the location of their combination home-school building. This building—a three-story house of 12 large rooms, three halls (each 10 by 40 feet) and four open porches—was considered one of the finest structures in that part of Alabama.

On January 1, 1871, Mars Hill Academy, the first Bible school in the South to be founded by a member of the church of Christ was opened to receive students. The school term began in January of each year and continued for 24 weeks. Most of the students were young men training to be preachers. A few young ladies attended for the purpose of learning to be better Bible school teachers. Perhaps no other school in Bible school history has had such a short life, yet wielded such great influence. "Larimore Boys" were prominent in various fields throughout the Southern states. The school was successfully managed for 17 years and only closed when T. B. Larimore felt he was neglecting the preaching of the gospel to lost souls.

Mrs. Larimore and their seven children continued to live in this home while Brother Larimore was away so much of the time until her death in 1907. The home was then converted into rental apartments and became a haven for many other families. Later Brother Larimore was married to Miss Emma Page, and he and his family moved to California where they spent their remaining years.

Approximately 75 years passed and another school came into being. In 1947 this new Mars Hill School opened its doors. At this time operation began in the original Larimore home and barn. The buildings which now house Mars Hill Bible School were erected in 1956. The kindergarten continued in the original home until 1968. The Mars Hill Bible School of today is an extension of the tradition of academic excellence, the development of the whole individual and the same philosophy of building for God and country.

While the expansion and growth of acres and buildings were being realized, the home itself was silently in retirement for about a decade. No one really seemed to notice or care. Finally the Associated Women's Organization for Mars Hill Bible School, a service organization working under the direction and supervision of the Board of Directors and Administration of the school, understood the significance of this old home. The call for restoration now came in the form of a challenge. This group of Christian women, welcoming the challenge, began a renewed effort toward trying to do something about THE LARIMORE HOUSE. Many were optimistic, many were hesitant and a few were just plainly scared.

In 1970, approximately 100 years from the time the house was built, the AWO shouldered the seemingly impossible financial and physical task of picking up the pieces and litereally putting the house back together again. It has been said that "old houses mended cost little less than new before they are ended." This building was in such ill repair after serving the needs of so many people for so many years that we hardly knew where or how to begin; but we did. WE HAD A MIND TO WORK.

Since it seemed the logical place to begin, we concentrated our efforts on the exterior of the building which was showing signs of fast, permanent deterioration. The following steps were undertaken:

1. All modifications to the original buildings including added stairways and other additions were removed.

2. New gutters and downspouts were installed.

3. Chimneys were repaired for safety.

4. All leaks were stopped.

5. The balcony-porches were reconstructed. (Much of the original mouldings, spindles, etc., were located and used.

With the feeling that much progress had been made, we then ventured inside to cope with the dilapidated interior of the main floor. All floors were sanded and finished, plastered walls were patched, wood trim stripped of so many coats of paint, fireplaces opened and mantles added.

On this second or main floor the walls are now papered with beautiful Williamsburg paper; woodwork and floors now glow with a beautiful sheen; and the light fixtures selected are in keeping with the architectural features recognized in the house. Many, many hours were spent and lots of loving care went into the redoing of this floor, especially the gracious stairway leading from the foyer to the third floor. As to the furnishings of this part of the house, we point with pride to the many family pieces which orginally had their niche in a particular corner all their own.

The four big rooms and hall of the third floor are restored to the point of now being used by the Associated Women's Organization for their meeting hall and work rooms. This part of the house will gradually return to its original use as need arises.

Now, follow me down the flight of worn steps which lead into the cellar area. The arrangement of rooms here is the same as the two floors above. We are told that the actual everyday chores of living went on right here in these spacious rooms. Much of the cooking was done over fireplace coals; the washing, ironing, canning and eating all took place right here a century ago.

We were happy to recognize the original basement floors as being Alabama limestone. (The same stone was used in the steps leading from both the front and back porches.) These stones were hauled by wagon from Smithsonia, the bend of the river, and set into their respective positions. They are in perfect condition today and serving the same purpose for which they were originally intended.

Much of the plaster on the walls had crumbled beyond repair, so the laborious task of literally "knocking the walls down" took place. All the loose plaster was removed, leaving the sections which were secure. Behind this plaster the original old bricks started peeping out. The walls were finished with a sealer and the remaining plastered portion was painted, with some walls being decorated with an old process called "stippling" Upon removal of the plasterboard ceiling in the hall the original beams emerged. The fireplaces were all cleaned and made safe for cheerful fires in each room.

The entire cellar creates a very nostalgic, rustic atmosphere. Cooking pots and pans have found their way to an old-fashioned wood stove, and a churn patiently sits beside the open fire awaiting its turn. One truly has the feeling of literally stepping back into the past and partaking of the good old days. The kitchen area has been fully equipped for use in preparing and serving delicious meals. The door of "Virgil's Cellar" swings ajar revealing wide open fireplaces, the fragrances of spices, homemade pickles and hot yeast rolls.

The cellar rooms have been named for various members of the Larimore family as follows:

```
Entire basement area ............................ Virgil's Cellar
Kitchen area ................................... Esther's Kitchen
Dining rooms.................................. Dedie's Cupboard
                                                 Ettie's Pantry
                                             Granville's Galley
Door leading upstairs
  points to..................................... T.B.'s Domain
```

The cellar is open Monday through Friday. Catered receptions, luncheons, dinners and teas are served by reservation only. Numbers of people enjoy Southern cooking and gracious hospitality here, with many of the recipes used today having been gleaned from the Larimore cookbooks and the kitchens of the entire Mars Hill community.

Please consider this to be your personal invitation to enjoy "a sentimental journey" visiting this historic shrine and seeing the beauty and dignity of the restored home.* This building is reminiscent of an era when the land was still fairly new and unsettled and New Testament Christianity was being attacked from all sides.

Virgil Larimore, the last of the Larimores, passed away December 30, 1972, at the age of 93. We are so happy that he seemed pleased with the restoration of his ancestral home. He visited the home several times and recommended it as an ideal place to eat a good meal amid the splendor and reminders of an illustrious past. In talking about his famous father he said, "I don't understand how my father did so much." We do—for we know he was truly about his Father's business.

There is something about our heritage that resists being bought and sold. Everything at the Larimore Home is a little bit special. It is

---

*In 1975 the Larimore Home was added to the Alabama and the National Historical Registers.

as special as the elusive and gracious spirit of southern hospitality waiti.ig
to welcome you as you make entrance to the peace and quiet of the north
veranda. The lovely wide porch offers big, old-fashioned rocking chairs
extending a gracious welcome. Each room of the home seems to be
anxious to tell its own particular story of joys, heartbreaks and sorrows.
All this has gone into making this house a home.

One is genuinely thrilled and inspired to see the beautiful old building
take on new life looking forward to another long and useful era. It has
truly been connected with ETERNITY from its beginning. It is today the
hub of activity at our Mars Hill Bible School. All the proceeds from
services derived from this house go toward the fulfillment of Brother
Larimore's dream, through us, for Christian education.

Grateful acknowledgement is made to: *Larimore and his Boys* by F. D.
Srygley, "World Evangelist," January, 1973, and all my friends and
co-workers at the Larimore Home.

WOMEN'S PLACE

In the beginning, God—
Assigned duties to all
Woman in her strength and love
Graciously answered her call

She took her place 'midst everyone
Awaiting the birth of her
infant son
Fitting snugly into her sphere
Loving her home, her husband
and children dear

The care of the world on her shoulders
seem to be given
Her's is the task of training and teaching
and leading to Heaven

Alma D. Biggs

The history of mankind reveals that since the beginning of time
women have been an important part of God's creation. Today women

are making headlines, and we are inclined to turn to the "society" section of our newspaper first in order to see who is doing what. We, as women, have now and have always had our place. We should strive to recognize this place and then to fit snugly and happily into our very own sphere.

Women

In the beautiful Garden of Eden
During God's eternal plan
Many creations appeared
But none suitable for man

From the treasury of God's mind
We see beauty and virtue
Like a flower—unwind
She stands proud and tall
But, alas! —the fateful Fall

The hope of the lost comes from above
God's grace showers us
With his love
He gave his Son—we honor and adore
Through this great gift
HE will

Restore—RESTORE

Alma D. Biggs

When God beheld the works of his hand, He declared them "good" and "very good." However, He soon realized that the man He had made from the dust of the earth needed a proper companion, and there was not found a helper suitable for him in all creation. God said, "It is not good that man should be alone," so He made woman and brought her unto him. Thus, a perfect woman—the climax of God's work—came into being.

Think how wonderful it would have been if this relationship with God could have remained as intended. From this perfect state the woman was soon to make a choice between right and wrong, between God and Satan. From the Bible story we know her ill-fated decision which caused mankind to be forced to live in a world filled with thorns and thistles, to earn bread by the sweat of their brow, and finally to return unto dust. Sin came into this beautiful world through the mistake of a woman, and through her God set into motion a plan for the hope of our RESTORATION.

Many times while visiting the hospital we peep into the nursery and whisper, "Aren't they sweet?" We use these words so casually with no special meaning except as a nice way to make conversation. One day on just such a visit, a little white crib near the window caught my eye. One could discern pretty cameo-like features and a quantity of hair, a tiny rosebud mouth, pink and white complexion and, as far as I could tell, a perfect little figure. This might have been your baby girl or my precious little granddaughter. Anyway, at that moment she was a beautiful specimen of God's handiwork! One could almost wish for time to stop so that this little life could always remain in this perfect state. But day by day this wee bit of femininity will grow and come face to face with her own joys, sorrows and heartaches which will prove to be just plain LIFE. Many times she will call out for love and understanding in order to complete the cycle from her perfect beginning to her eternal perfection or RESTORA-TION. Go with me now in your mind as we follow this lovely child in the various stages of life.

A little girl has a beginning like a flower with her true beauty waiting to be unfolded. This beauty and charm will blossom forth if given an opportunity through a childhood nourished with love and harmony. These first months and years of her life should be devoted to making her feel wanted and loved and to the discovery of God's beautiful world.

We have been reminded so many times that the personality of a child is fairly well established in its very early years. The Catholic people have long been saying, "Give us a child until the age of 6 or 7 and we will hand you a Catholic for life." This rule has proven true not only regarding religious beliefs but regarding many other aspects of a child's life. The old saying, "Like mother, like daughter," is very true. A little girl will follow in the footsteps of mother and grandmother, so we must walk carefully and prayerfully lest we lead in the wrong direction.

A few years pass and she is no longer a baby. She has entered the world of school, clubs, secret pals, Girl Scouts, etc. There can be no doubt of the influence of the home during this important period. Though I am now a grandmother, sometimes I wish I could turn back the pages of time to when I was a young mother. Like so many others, I readily admit to things I would do differently. I was reared during depression and

therefore had very few advantages that would with the stretch of
imagination be called luxuries. Therefore, I, like many other mothers, felt
that my husband and I must provide THINGS for our children. We were
trying to relive our lives in the young ones around us. Wouldn't it be
wonderful if we could be as wise during the trying years of rearing as we
think we are today in the evening of our lives? I now realize that it is not
nearly so important to have THINGS as to have a proper relationship
with oneself and with God. "What shall it profit a man, if he shall gain
the whole world, and lose his own soul?" (Mark 8:36). Today is the time
to show this precious little girl by example the love and loveliness of
Christ.

Somewhere during this growing-up process you suddenly realize that
the little girl in pigtails is thinking for herself. She has been taught about
Christ and His Church. The plan of salvation is imprinted upon her
heart. Now she and she alone, like Eve, must make a choice of servitude.
She ponders the question, "Whom will I serve—God or man?" We are all
so happy when we witness her obedience by confession and baptism to
become a new creature in Christ Jesus. Today she stands pure and sinless.
Now, she is launching out on the highway that leads to the eternal
city of God—toward that perfect RESTORATION. She has accepted the
responsibility for others to join hands with her and through faith, prayer
and work her life from now on will be a dedicated service.

Dear Sweet Sixteen: You will soon be graduating, and your thoughts
are turning to romance. There are so many things that could be said right
here and so much advice that could come from the experienced that you
might or might not heed, but we cannot create a set pattern for you.
This is your life, not like any other that has ever been lived, and you
must direct your own steps. Prepare the garden of your life carefully and
prayerfully, for "where you tend a rose, a thistle cannot grow." Fill your
mind with springtime and the beauty of simple, uncluttered living. It is
natural for you to look forward to being an independent adult and going
out on your own, but just live one minute at a time. Be happy and enjoy
this beautiful time of your life. Just mere thoughts are as good for you
as sunlight or as bad as any destructive power. To let unclean thoughts
take haven in your mind is dangerous and can corrupt your whole
attitude. Cultivate and exercise the great blessings of love. Let
1 Corinthians 13 become an altar of your heart.

Pray for God's guidance and be patient and one day the right one for
you will come along. Be sure he is a Christian, for God says He is not
pleased if his child is unequally yoked with an unbeliever. Two people

striving to put Christ first in their lives is the foundation upon which to build a happy home.

Time passes swiftly, and we love you as you say the words, "I do," and "till death do us part." You are a lovely young woman and can be likened to a full-blown rose. You know now that marriage is not only a ceremony but a new and beautiful experience for a man and woman to become one in the blending of their lives together. Marriage always demands more sacrifice than we could have imagined. You've heard that marriages are made in heaven, but they must be worked at right here at home. You are not flawless, and neither is the one you promised to love and cherish. With hard work, patience and most of all with God's help your marriage can become what you want it to be. It is within your sphere to create a happy home.

You were not only placed side by side with your husband to be his companion and helper but also the mother of his children. It takes the patter of little feet and the trusting cling of a small hand to make a family complete. A little child is a gift from God which should someday be returned to him bearing the characteristics of love, care and protection.

> God loaned this child to me
> I pray that I will worthy be
> To watch o'er her both day and night
> and guide her footsteps in the right.

It seems now as you have reached the middle years of your life that it is the most apprehensive time. Your child has grown up and you are tense with fear that she will falter. Like mother, like daughter you have taught her God's ways to the best of your ability. You must be patient and pray that she will remember her Creator. You are no different from any other mother, for we all have sleepless nights. Yet, we must take courage and hope in the scripture that tells us to "Train up a child in the way he should go: and when he is old, he will not depart from it" (Proverbs 22:6 RSV).

How sweet is the word, "mother," for in it is embraced all that is pure and holy, good and beautiful. We linger over it with tenderness and enshrine it in our hearts like a precious jewel to be guarded and prized as long as life shall last. From a mother's loving influence emanates all that is ennobling and that inspires us with longings after a higher and better life. Who can estimate the value of a mother's influence or measure the depths of her love? They are links between us and heaven.

Today, your body is beginning to show signs of wear. It is a burden to you. You are eagerly awaiting that new body, free from pain. You know it is far better to depart and be with the Lord. You pray for strength to look after your own needs and not be a burden to others.

Are you waiting for Christ to come? "Behold, I am coming soon, bringing my recompense, to repay every one for what he has done. I am the Alpha and the Omega, the first and the last, the beginning and the end. Blessed are those who wash their robes, that they may have the right to the tree of life and that they may enter the city by the gates" (Revelation 22:12-14 RSV).

As you make preparation for the last and final journey, many things enter into your planning. It is much like journeying into a foreign country. First you must learn about the country to which you are to go. You need a guide to tell you the value of the places and things to be visited, etc. In God's Word He promises there will be no want, no suffering and no pain. He will wipe away all tears. Who would not desire a home such as this?

The chief aim of life from the cradle to the grave is to glorify God and enjoy Him forever. Paul said in 1 Corinthians 10:31, "Whether you eat or drink, or whatever you do, do all to the glory of God" (RSV). The purpose of life is not an endless pursuit of pleasure but rather a search for meaning in the midst of mystery. From Jesus Christ we have a clue to the meaning of that mystery—"Seek ye first the kingdom of God, and his righteousness; and all these things shall be added unto you" (Matthew 6:33).

Daughters, mothers, and grandmothers—regardless of where you are standing now—at this very minute, redeem your time. If you have continued in the faith until death, you will be gathered together with God, Christ, the Holy Spirit and all the redeemed. Yours will again be perfection, the circle unbroken, a complete RESTORATION of God's most beautiful creation.

SOULS

Out of the depths have I cried unto thee, O Lord
Lord, hear my voice: let thine ears be attentive to the voice of
      my supplications.
If thou, Lord, shouldest mark iniquities, O Lord, who shall stand?
      But there is forgiveness with thee, that thou mayest
      be feared.
I wait for the Lord, my SOUL doth wait, and in his word do I hope.
My SOUL waiteth for the Lord more than they that watch for the
      morning; I say, more than they that watch for the morning.
Let Israel hope in the Lord: for with the Lord there is mercy, and
      with him is plenteous redemption.
And he shall redeem Israel from all his iniquities.

Psalm 130

"And the Lord God formed man of the dust of the ground, and breathed into his nostrils the breath of life; and man became a living soul" (Genesis 2:7). In Genesis 6:6, ". . .it repented the Lord that he had made man on the earth, and it grieved him at his heart." God created all men as free agents—free to accept or reject Christ as they themselves determine. In the early lives of Adam and Eve this freedom was exercised, and mankind has forever been thought of as "fallen man." But God was so concerned about the everlasting soul of man that He immediately unfolded a plan whereby man may have eternal life—not as a tarnished, sinful human being but as a perfectly cleansed soul prepared for heaven. "The Lord is merciful and gracious, slow to anger and plenteous in mercy" (Psalm 103:8).

We are God's children, and He has been mindful of us just as we are mindful of our own children. How many of us would provide stones for our own instead of food? God looked down the stream of time and insured our future upon the condition that we meet his specifications. We might liken this great gift to the feeling of parents concerned as to the security of their children after they can no longer be there to encourage or provide. God reminded Israel over and over in the long ago that as long as his chosen people walked with Him that He would be in their midst. God reminds us today in the Christian dispensation that He is the author of eternal salvation and has commanded that all men should repent. "The Lord is not slack concerning his promise, as some men count slackness; but is long-suffering to us-ward, not willing that any should perish, but that all should come to repentance'' (2 Peter 3:9).

When Christ arose and ascended to be with God, weak and frail humanity was not left here to the wiles of evil influences, but our hope of salvation was placed in earthen vessels. The Holy Spirit through the Word of God makes clear the path that all men must follow in order to reach the eternal city. We have not earned salvation by our own goodness and works but only through the grace of God through Jesus Christ his Son.

All souls must be restored if they are to be acceptable to God. For too long we have waited for lost souls to come to this realization on their own, but God's Word teaches us that we must arise and go to them. The message we must bring is this:

1. The gospel is God's power to save.

2. God is no respector of persons; the gospel is for all.

3. Once we have the gospel, we must share it.

Our soul may be compared to the shipment of a precious gift. Since we know that the highway is straight, narrow and rough we stamp the warning, "Fragile, handle with care," on our package. This same precaution should be given our soul on its journey down the highway of life because the everlasting part of man must also be given proper care. Our journey begins the day we are born and we plod along until our last day upon this earth. "Then shall the dust return to the earth as it was: and the spirit shall return unto God who gave it" (Ecclesiastes 12:7). Without proper handling our soul will be delivered to judgment battered and damaged.

What price tag can we put on this important cargo, our soul?

1. It is worth more than the whole world (Mark 8:36-37).

2. God gave up his only Son in behalf of it (John 3:16, Romans 5:8).

3. Jesus humbled himself, suffered and died to save it (Matthew 1:21, Luke 19:10).

4. It is so dear that Jesus is preparing a place in heaven for it (John 14:1-4).

A great writer once said, God has given a man two eyes. If he should lose one he has another, but he has only one soul. If he should lose that, it can never be regained.

Christ said that He had gone to prepare a place for a prepared people. Once we enter the doors of the heavenly city and hear the greeting, "Well done, thou good and faithful servant:. . .enter thou into the joy of thy lord," we will know that the soul has at least been RESTORED and will be placed at the right hand of God, an heir of God and joint-heir of Christ. The blessings of joy and happiness beyond comprehension have been held in trust for us until this time.

Mrs. Alma Biggs
829 River Bluff Terrace
Sheffield, Alabama

SUCCESSES
AND
FAILURES
IN REARING CHILDREN

"Lo, children are a heritage of the Lord: and the fruit of the womb is his reward" (Psalms 127:3).

One of the greatest blessing ever bestowed upon woman is that of rearing children. This blessing is accompanied with awesome responsibility. When that tiny little bundle is first placed in a mother's arms, it is as though God is saying, "Here is a soul I am intrusting to your care. Train it well, because where it spends eternity will largely depend upon you."

The godly mother produces a better product than any factory, farm or plant. Abraham Lincoln once said, "All that I am, or can be, I owe to my angel mother." Augustine said, "Give me mothers that are mothers and I will change the world." "Men are what their mothers make them" (Emerson). "The hand that rocks the cradle is the hand that rules the world" (William Wallace). An old Spanish proverb says, "An ounce of mother is worth a pound of clergy." Henry W. Beecher once commented, "The mother's heart is the child's schoolroom." And Simmons wrote, "If you would reform the world from its errors and vices, begin by enlightening its mothers." Indeed we need real, genuine dedicated mothers!

As a mother of four children (one of whom departed this life January 3, 1974), I have had a multiplicity of experiences. But not for one moment do I claim or feel that I know all the answers. I readily admit many failures.

35

It has been said, "If you really want some good advice on rearing children, just ask an old maid or someone who has never had children." Most people, I will agree, are more free with advice before they have children. I had a lot of set rules before my children were born. I soon learned that my rules were flexible, and sometimes even broken. Now this is not to conclude that we should not have rules and regulations. We must have. I am saying that sometimes things just do not go the way we had hoped.

Those of us who have more than one child know that what may prove successful for one child will not necessarily be just right for another. Some parents seem not to have learned this fact, for they just cannot understand why their children react so differently. One may be heard to say, "I have treated them exactly alike." We must realize that every human being has a different personality. God made it so. Therefore, we must accept each child for what he is and avoid making comparisons.

Teach Them God's Word

All Christian parents agree that their children should be taught the Word of God. No doubt, many who do not profess Christianity would agree this is right and good. Paul writing to Timothy in 2 Timothy 1:5 said, "When I call to remembrance the unfeigned faith that is in thee, which dwelt first in thy grandmother Lois, and thy mother Eunice, and I am persuaded that in thee also." This verse teaches us that the kind of faith we have not only affects our children but will affect our grandchildren. Therefore, as parents we must study God's word in order to acquire the kind of faith that will help us in rearing our children (Romans 10:17). Paul also said of Timothy, "And that from a child thou hast known the holy scriptures, which are able to make thee wise unto salvation through faith which is in Christ Jesus" (2 Timothy 3:15). Mothers, can you think of anything that you would rather have someone say about a child of yours? What more could we want than for our children to know God's word and have the kind of faith that will make them wise unto salvation.

> Before your child has come to seven,
> teach him well the way to heaven.
> Better still the truth will thrive,
> if he knows it when he is only five.

Best of all is when you've begun,
to teach him Jesus before he is one.

The Biblical concept of the Lord's church is a must in the proper training of children. Do not keep your babies away from the place of worship because you feel they are too young to learn. A child is a precious and wonderful gift of God. For parents to neglect to take him to the place where he can learn and be trained to worship God is a grave error. Instead of being an excuse for forsaking the worship assemblies of the saints, a baby is another good reason for being faithful.

Parents who forsake the assembly when their child is a baby may say when the child is older that they do not take him because he just will not sit still and be quiet. Let me urge you to begin now to train that little one.

Most of us parents have had embarrasing experiences with our children during a worship service. Such disruptive action from them as tossing a doll two rows back, talking out loud or singing when nobody else is singing make us wonder at times, "Why did I come?" But thank God there are parents who are willing to keep trying, because they love the Lord and know the Bible teaches that we are to worship in spirit and in truth. A pattern is being set, and the child that is hardest to manage may someday preach the gospel! Some people may stare at you and even wish you were not there but if you are doing the best you can to train the child, God is pleased. Make sure you are doing the best that you can, though, to keep the child quiet, so others will not be disturbed who are worshipping God. Parents should be commended who are bringing their children because they want them to grow up with a strong, enduring faith in God and His Word.

Start while they are young to have a set time for devotional periods. Teach them to pray. Hearing you pray is a good way for them to learn. A little boy once said to his father, "Daddy, is God dead?" The father replied, "No, why did you ask such a question as that?" "Well, I haven't heard you talking to him lately," answered the boy.

Show Them the Way

Each day we write a letter, as it were, to our children by what we say and do. Those trusting little eyes see everything we do. For the first few years they believe that their parents can do most anything. Our

Timothy had great confidence in his father. Once when he was very small
and in his daddy's arms he looked at the new moon and said, "Daddy
the moon is broke; fix it." Those are happy years. Of course we parents
should not deceive our little ones by making them think we are perfect.
Think of the contrast. When they get to be teenagers they feel that
parents know almost nothing.

If we really want to be successful in rearing our children we will take
time to train them. This is a full time job, but it is worth every effort
that one can muster. One should look at his little one and think, "I am
training this child for eternity."

The way you teach is important and what you teach is important, but
how you live is most important in the training of your children. It is
unthinkable to expect a child to listen to your advice and ignore your
example. A man once told his children, "Don't do as I do, but do as I
say." This is contrary to the teaching of Jesus. Jesus began both to do
and to teach. I want to follow someone who is willing to be an example,
not only in word but in deed also. I want my children to follow my
example only as I follow the example of Christ.

Show them how to have a good time. There are many ways for
children to have good and wholesome fun. Christians should be the
happiest people in the world. Someone has said that Christians should be
cheerful and not go around with such long faces that they look like
they could eat oats out of a churn. It is easy to be cheerful when
things are going our way, but the way we act when the going gets rough
is the true test of our actions.

Discipline Properly

When we think of the relationship of children to parents, we
immediately think of Ephesians 6:1-3. "Children, obey your parents in
the Lord: for this is right. Honour thy father and mother; (which is the
first commandment with promise;) that it may be well with thee, and thou
mayest live long on the earth." This passage clearly shows that children
must be obedient to their parents in order to please God but obedience
is also necessary for the following reasons:

1. The good order of a family depends upon it.

2. The welfare of the child depends upon it.

3. The child is not competent, as yet, to reason what is right or qualified to direct himself.

4. The parents by virtue of age and experience are more capable of directing the child.

God in His infinite wisdom knew that for a family to have good order there must of necessity be the proper respect for authority. If we parents do not teach our children to be obedient to us, we cannot expect them to be obedient to their teachers at school, or in Sunday school, or to the laws of the land.

Children love to please; therefore, look for the good things they do and compliment them. Do not dwell on their mistakes. Many mistakes will be made, but remember they are learning. Corrections should be made when mistakes occur, but without nagging. By admiration meted out to our children, their confidence in their ability to do things is strengthened. Children will go out of their way to get praise. Have you ever heard, "See me do it!" or "See what me made?" I have put many blossoming weeds in vases because my little ones had loved me enough to gather them and bring them to me. I can visualize that little tot with a smiling face and an outstretched hand that held a weed saying, "Look Mommy, I brought you a flower." As I looked into those loving eyes, that little weed suddenly became the most beautiful flower. Show sincere appreciation for every kind word or deed that they show you.

"And, ye fathers, provoke not your children to wrath: but bring them up in the nurture and admonition of the Lord" (Ephesians 6:4). How can fathers provoke their children to wrath? It is done by unreasonable commands, by needless severity, by the manifestation of anger. This command was addressed to fathers, because the father is the head of the family, and its government is especially on his shoulders. But this does not mean that we mothers do not need to study and think about this command.

Try to govern and punish your children in a way that they will not lose respect and confidence in you but will know that, because of the love that you have for them, you are trying to train them as you should. Instructions should be reasonable and such that can be obeyed. When we discipline a child it should not be when or because we are angry, but because we want to teach him to do right. One man told his son,

"I am going to slap you if you do not quit that," and then slapped him while he was making the remark. This is not the right way to discipline a child. I heard of the little boy who after being put to bed repeatedly asked his father to bring him a drink. The father thought the son just wanted attention. He finally told the little fellow, "If you ask for a drink again, I'm going after a switch." In a few minutes the boy said, "Daddy, when you go after that switch, please stop by the faucet and get me a drink of water."

"The rod and reproof give wisdom: but a child left to himself bringeth his mother to shame" (Proverbs 29:15).

Give of Your Time

Many parents try to give their children "things" that their parents were unable to give them. Some fathers spend much time away from home and family desperately trying to make enough money to supply all the luxuries that the family wants. It is not good when the father is gone from the family so much. The children miss much by not having him around, and he even misses more by not being with them. We often see mothers leave their little ones and take a job. Sometimes this may be necessary, but in a lot of cases it is just to have more "things." When this desire is the reason for working, I feel it is a mistake. Some children are left in good care and with proper supervision, but others are not. In some cases there is no one at home when the children get home from school. They always seem to want to see mother after having been away from her all day. When they open the door and discover that mother is not there to answer when they call, it is a very lonely, frustrating feeling. The scripture teaches, "A man's life consisteth not in the abundance of the things which he possesseth" (Luke 12:15). If at all possible it is wise for the mother to stay home and train her children. Someone has so aptly said, "The greatest gift a father can give his children is their mother's time."

You may say, "I do not want my child to work as hard as I had to work." Or perhaps you feel that it is easier and faster to go ahead yourself and wash the dishes, make the beds, vacuum the floors, dust, take out the garbage, etc., instead of assigning some of these tasks to your children. Both these attitudes encourage laziness in children and are unfair. Begin when they are young to teach them to work. Mothers need to take the time to teach daughters to cook and perform other household tasks, so they will not be at a loss when they have the responsibility of a home of their own. Likewise, boys should be taught to be responsible and to engage in their share of the work. When a boy reaches manhood and marries, it is his responsibility to be head of the house, and therefore, the work of providing for the family rests mainly on his shoulders. If he has been taught to work from childhood and taught to do each menial task well, then the responsibility of caring for a household will not be so frightening.

We have our children at home with us for such a short time. Someone has said, "The trouble with being a parent is that by the time you are experienced, you are unemployed." We are such busy mothers that we sometimes do not take enough time to really enjoy our children. Housework is a full time job, and some mothers get so engrossed "doing things" that the most important job is overlooked, namely molding a life for eternity. Consider the advice of two mothers in two different situations.

A Message From a Deacon's Wife

"I am the mother of two boys, ages 4 and 8. Since my husband works on afternoon shift, it falls my lot to share most of their study time as well as play time. Afternoons were a busy time for me. When the boys would come in and beg me to come out and pitch ball or sit down and read a book, I found myself saying, 'I'll do it later,' and later would not come. There would be homework, meals to prepare, baths and bedtime. Soon they were asleep, and it was too late. Once in awhile I would almost grudgingly leave my work, telling them all the time that I didn't have time, and all during the game that I had to get back to my work.

"Then one day I read an article in a woman's magazine that opened my eyes. It was written by a busy mother. It appeared that her problems and lack of time were similar to mine, but she had worked out a solution. If she were really busy with work that could not be dropped when her children came in asking her to share their play, she would tell them a time when she would be through and could come out and play with them. When that time came, she put everything else aside and played or shared with them, giving them her full, happy attention. When the play time was over, she could then go back to her work.

"I began to try this. A time was set aside for homework and a time for recreation. This was not an overnight success, but gradually the children began to understand and really appreciate the time we spent together. I could see a big change in their attitude. I believe they could see a greater change in mine. It became a time to plan for, and soon we were including weekends and times that daddy was home also. I took time to pitch and bat balls, try roller skating, collect football cards, sit down and watch ball games, read books, go to the library, fill swimming pools, build sand castles and many other things. I found that I really enjoyed doing these things because I was doing them with my family. I learned that children can understand time being set aside for certain things. What they cannot understand is a promise broken or never fulfilled.

"I am thankful to say that now my boys and I share a lot of happy times together. Mothers can be just as close to their boys as their girls in different ways. I think every mother who does not make time for her children is missing something very valuable, namely childhood. All too soon it is gone, never to be seen again—except in memory."

Martha Montgomery

A Message From a Nurse

"Webster says success is 'a favorable result.' To me success in rearing children is having a goal and working to reach it. You cannot put a tray in the refrigerator and come back later to find a nice dinner on it. You must plan a meal and make your plan work. This need of a goal is so much greater in rearing children.

"As blood-bought Christians we must have heaven as our goal for our children. Everything they do must be centered around this hope. Where they go, what they watch on T. V., how they dress, who their friends are, and every aspect of living must daily be compared to what Christ our Lord would want. In the law of Moses parents were instructed to teach their children while they were sitting, standing, walking and lying down (Deuteronomy 11:19-21).

"Personally, I do not feel I can claim success. My goal for my children is heaven. They are all Christians now, and I thank God for this; but there is a life to be lived by each of them, and eternity alone will tell the outcome. I believe each of my children loves God. A child taught to love God very early in his life is given a foundation for every storm he has to face. When everything around him is shakey, he can hold on to his love for God, for no one can take this from him.

"Failure? Yes, I admit failure many times. Hardly a day goes by that I don't look back and see immaturity, weak spirituality, lack of wisdom and lack of knowledge on my part. I must then come face to face with the fact that my children have been touched by my weakness. I have often said that my children are what they are in spite of me, not because of me. Three things I wish I could go back and try to do over: (1) use my time more wisely, (2) be less critical and more complimentary and (3) be more aware of the example I am setting each day. Also, I would face difficulties with less fright and more faith, because I have found that one teaches children very little by just talking to them. By the time they can understand what parents are saying, they have already learned a way of life by the actions of the parents."

Patsy Pepper

Love Them Fervently

The chief ingredient for a happy home is love. Every individual has a basic desire to be needed and loved. We need love from the time we draw our first breath. It is a true saying that love is a good medicine. We call it T. L. C.—tender loving care. Deprive a baby of love and soon the physical being will become affected. The reassurance of love often has a profound effect on the physically or mentally ill.

Parents set the stage for love in the home. Frequent demonstrations of love of parents for each other and for their children will cultivate happy, well-adjusted children. They will learn to give love themselves. Love is reciprocal—the more you give your children, the more they give you in return. Love pays big dividends. Have you ever had the experience of putting your child to bed, hearing his prayer, and then having him hug you and say, "You are the best mother in the world!"?

Love is so abundant for some, and yet others are starving for it. We have all seen children who act in such a way that it is hard to love them. They may even tell you that they do not want or need love or friends. The truth more than likely is that they are so starved for love that they have become embittered. Keep before your children at all times the happiness that you feel because they are your children. Never make them feel in the way or unwanted.

Show no partiality in dealing with your children. Love each one for what he is. Some children are more physically attractive than others, but remember God looks on the heart. Teach children to like and accept themselves because they are made in the very image of God. They should concern themselves with developing their own God-given abilities and talents.

We are happy when our children show love for us, but let them know that love for God must come first (Matthew 10:37). The death of my son, Timothy, at age 26 brought home the importance to me of this teaching. It seems that we had him for such a short while. I know now that of all the things his father and I taught him from the time he was born until the time he left us, nothing we taught him was more important than teaching him to love God and keep his commandments. From having taught him these truths, we feel assured that some day we will be reunited with him to spend an eternity together in God's great, beautiful city. We thank God for this hope. Parents, I must urge you to be serious about preparing your children to be ready to die and meet God. My husband has written of the death of the righteous:

> Death's a kiss of peace
> When facing eternity's door
> We pass with fond release
> Where frailties vex no more.

Christian parents have no greater opportunity for good than the opportunity to develop their children. Daniel Webster said, "If we work upon marble, it will perish; if we work upon brass, time will efface it; if we rear temples, they will crumble into dust; but if we work upon immortal souls, if we endow them with principles; with the just fear of the Creator and love of fellowman, we engrave on those tablets something which will brighten all Eternity."

Mrs. Margie Overton
Route 9, Box 547
Florence, Alabama

MAKING LIFE WORTHWHILE

"Heaven is a surer heritage if we make this life worthwhile."
George Elliot

If we have the ability to enjoy life we make it worthwhile for ourselves and others. According to Webster, worthwhile means "being worth the time spent; of sufficient value to repay the effort." Therefore, to make our lives worthwhile we must use the time that has been given us to the best advantage and see that each day something has been accomplished to make that day useful or valuable and not just wasted hours. When we have learned to fill our days with worthwhile things, we will have added that plus that makes the true Christian above average.

Jesus certainly is our supreme example of a worthwhile life. He made every minute count for something. I feel quite sure He did not waste time or idle away hours daydreaming about what might be or dwelling on the past. We can cultivate this same zeal for life that the Master had. It will cost us though, in comfort, time and energy. It cost Jesus his very life.

Some people drift through life without any purpose or aim. They have nothing in particular to do, nothing in particular to interest them and no opinion worth listening to. They aim at nothing and reach it. No one should value life so lightly and make life so worthless.

Too many people try to live in the past or in the future, and they miss all the joys that the present has to offer. Read Paul's philosophy in Philippians 3:13-14: "Brethren, I do not regard myself as having laid hold of it yet; but one thing I do:forgetting what lies behind and reaching forward to what lies ahead I press on toward the goal for the prize of the upward call of God in Christ Jesus" (NASB). Our goals must be the right ones and ones that have been made with God and His will for our life in mind. A Christian's main goal should be to serve God and keep his commandments (Ecclesiastes 12:13). In 1 John 5:2-5 we read that God's commandments are not burdensome and that by our faith we can overcome the world and its cares. If we keep busy doing God's will there will be no time for idleness, worry or any of the other things that can sap one's strength and energy. We can encourage others by our confidence and obedience to God's will.

Remember the good old song that says, "What's the use of worrying? It never was worthwhile. So pack up your troubles in your old kit-bag and smile, smile, smile." These words were written by George Asaf about 60 years ago and they are very good advice today. Of all the things you wear, your expression is the most important. The next time you catch a glimpse of yourself in a store window or a counter mirror, skip the glance at your necklace or your hair-do and look at what is between them. Then decide if it isn't worth a little time and effort to exchange that look of grim determination or worry for something a little more appealing, a look that could help convince yourself and others that you are living a life worthwhile.

Worry will never get you anywhere and will sap your strength and desire to do worthwhile things. Everyone has times when they have extra concern about someone or something, but we should pray and ask God to help us do what we can and then go on to other things. "Be anxious for nothing but in everything by prayer and supplication with thanksgiving let your requests be made known to God. And the peace of God, which surpasses all comprehension, shall guard your hearts and your minds in Christ Jesus" (Philippians 4:6-7 NASB). Worry ruins the present, cannot change the past and does not help the future. Our prayer should be: "God grant me the serenity to accept the things I cannot change; courage to change the things I can; and wisdom to know the difference."

One fine lady recommends that you put cards with the word, "Enjoy," on them in every room in the house. When you see these reminders, you will try to enjoy and be happy about whatever you are doing— whether it be washing dishes, scrubbing floors or some other job that is not your favorite. You are doing these menial but essential tasks for your family, for those you love. Before you know it, your so-called chores will be finished and you will be free to pursue other activities. "This is the day which the Lord hath made; we will rejoice and be glad in it" (Psalms 118:24).

A worthwhile life will be spent in service to others—family, friends or strangers—whoever happens to need our help. In Matthew 20:26b-28 Jesus tells us, "But whoever wishes to become great among you shall be your slave; just as the Son of Man did not come to be served, but to serve, and to give His life a ransom for many" (NASB). So abundant are the ways in which we can serve that we should never have to sit and wait for someone to assign us a job. The sick and shut-ins appreciate cheerful visits or cards. Many people could use our help with chores that they are unable to do because of health or other reasons. Those who do not drive need transportation to various places. The church is always in need of those who are willing to teach classes, do personal work and many other Christian services.

When we have lived our lives and are ready to leave this world, we will stand before the judgment seat of God. God will not ask us, "Why were you not Moses, Joshua, John or Paul?" or "Why were you not Lydia, Dorcas, Mary or Sarah?" He will perhaps ask us very simply, "Why were you not Joan Banks, doing the things set for you and no one else?" Many times we depend on others to make a better life for us while we do nothing in return. Daily sacrifice becomes pleasure if made for those who are dear to us. We must learn to renounce self; each act of self-denial is a rung of a ladder by which we climb nearer to heaven.

Everyone is in such a rush today that the small courtesies are being forgotten. Do you remember to say, "Thank you"? The simple showing of appreciation is important. People are constantly helping us, influencing us or giving us things, and we seldom let them know how grateful we are.

A life worthwhile is nearly always a life of "little things." I feel quite certain that nobody ever lived who, without previous thought or training, turned the world upside down in only one day. It takes a lifetime of little deeds, little sacrifices and little tasks.

Our earliest task toward a life worthwhile is to learn obedience to our parents. Then before we know it, we expect this of our own children. We must begin early in our children's lives to train them so that they will be obedient—not only to us but to all other forms of authority. Many parents today seem to feel that someone else is going to teach their child the basic courtesies and attitudes of life. Because of this there are many children and young people who care only for themselves and have

little interest or consideration for others or the property of others. We
have our children such a short time that it is one of the worst tragedies
of humanity to blow our chance at helping to make their lives worthwhile
by bringing them up to have love and respect and to desire service.
We need to instill in both ourselves and our children the attitude
expressed in this poem by George Linnaeus Banks:

Why Do I Live?

I live for those who love me,
   For those I know are true,
For the heaven that smiles above me
   And awaits my spirit too;
For all human ties that bind me,
For the task my God assigned me,
For the bright hope left behind me,
   And the good that I can do.

I live to hold communion
   With all that is divine,
To feel that there is union
   'Twixt nature's heart and mind;
To profit by affliction.
Reap truth from fields of fiction,
Grow wiser from conviction,
   Fulfilling God's design.

I live for those who love me,
   For those I know are true,
For the heaven that smiles above me
   And awaits my spirit too;
For wrongs that need resistance,
For the cause that needs assistance,
For the future in the distance,
   And the good that I can do.

Used by permission from Leroy
Brownlow, *Flowers That Never Fade*,
Brownlow Publications

In our concern for our children and for others we must not forget
our husbands. Some of our time and attention belongs to them. Their

needs must be met before whatever activities we plan. Do we take the time to dress and look our best for them at home as well as when we are going out? Time spent each day in talking, listening and otherwise doing things together will be worthwhile for both husband and wife.

God's arrangement for man and woman is clearly given in 1 Corinthians 11:3: "But I want you to understand that Christ is the head of every man, and the man is the head of the woman, and God is the head of Christ" (NASB). If we will only let things be the way God planned we will be happier. It's hard for women today to remember to be in subjection, for so much is being done to try to give her more power. In the marriage relationship especially we must remember our own special role, so that it can be said of us, "The heart of her husband doth safely trust in her, so that he shall have no need of spoil. She will do him good and not evil all the days of her life" (Proverbs 31:11-12).

To be able to do all of the things that are being discussed in this chapter a person must keep in good physical condition. If you do not eat correctly and get the proper amount of rest, you will not be a cheerful person and will not be able to be busy. If you are grouchy and complaining, people will not want to be around you. Proverbs 18:24 tells us that if we want friends, we will have to show a friendly attitude ourselves. Friends are one of life's greatest blessings, and we all want to cultivate and keep our old friends and be making new ones all the time. Having someone in your home for a meal or refreshments is one of the best ways to get to know them.

We must accept the Bible and its truths as the basis on which to build a worthwhile life. Leroy Brownlow in his book, *Flowers That Never Fade* compiled a list of scriptures which he called "My Rules for Life." What better rules could we possibly use for a pattern? They are listed here, with his permission, in the hope that they will be a help to you.

1. Whatsoever ye would that men should do to you, do ye even so to them. (Matthew 7:12).
2. Recompense to no man evil for evil (Romans 12:17).
3. Follow after the things which make for peace (Romans 14:19).
4. Study to be quiet, and to do your own business, and to work with your hands (1 Thessalonians 4:11).
5. Make no friendship with an angry man (Proverbs 22:24).
6. Provide things honest in the sight of all men (Romans 12:17).
7. Be swift to hear, slow to speak, slow to wrath (James 1:19).

8. Buy the truth, and sell it not (Proverbs 22:23).
9. Love not sleep, lest thou come to poverty (Proverbs 20:13).
10. Whatsoever thy hand findeth to do, do it with thy might (Ecclesiastes 9:10).
11. Be ye thankful (Colossians 3:15).
12. Fear God, and keep his commandments, for this is the whole duty of man (Ecclesiastes 12:13).

All doors that lead to the worthwhile life are doors outward—out of self, out of smallness and out of wrong.

Mrs. Joan Banks
1702 33rd Street
Sheffield, Alabama

THE SIN
OF
INGRATITUDE

Many people whom we loved dearly have fallen victim to cancer, that dreaded, most feared disease. Perhaps you have had the same experience. How terrible it is to watch someone close to you be struck down and stripped of any semblance of dignity or normal appearance. When you are forced to sit by and watch while they slowly and painfully wither away, you wonder which is worse—the physical pain or the mental anguish.

Think about someone in particular who died or is dying of cancer. It is my honest opinion and belief that the person would give anything he owned or could borrow or beg to be healed of his affliction. I just don't believe there is a person living who would choose cancer as his way to leave this world.

What then do you think would happen if in a miraculous way he could be healed? Made whole! Completely cured of advanced cancer! "Why," you say, "that person would never get through thanking his benefactor." Perhaps not. I would certainly hope so. But do you know that according to Bible arithmetic if ten people were healed of advanced cancer, only one would have the kind of spirit in his heart to reach out his hand and say, "Thank you." This attitude is hard to accept but it is true. Most people suffer daily from the *sin of ingratitude*.

"Were not ten cleansed? Where are the nine? Was no one found to return and give praise to God except this foreigner?" (Luke 17:17 RSV). Here were 10 men who were suffering from a loathsome disease. The flesh was rotting on their bones. So repulsive were they that they were social outcasts and so dangerous to touch that men shrank from their shadow. History tells us that leprosy would actually be worse than cancer, because a leper was cast out from his friends and family to suffer and die alone.

Jesus healed all ten of these men of this terrible disease, but only one returned to give thanks. What do you suppose happened to the other nine? *Ingratitude!* It is a sin, and God doesn't like it. Surely God must be greatly disappointed when, surrounded by his rich blessings, we go about complaining because we don't have more. Romans 1:21 tells us just what importance God places on ingratitude. "They glorified him not as God, neither were they thankful. . . ." Next to the failure to worship God is the sin of ingratitude. If you can't have everything you'd like, try liking everything you have. Be thankful! There is a grave danger in not being thankful for the blessings we receive.

God has given us so many gifts, is giving them continually and will continue as long as we live. Last year's acorns still lie half-buried beneath the dead leaves. They wait with their cups uplifted to catch those few drops of rain that will nourish them and make them sprout and grow into mighty oaks lending shelter for passers-by. We must keep that cell of thankfulness open continually to fill to overflowing so that it might take root and grow upward toward God. If our cells are always ready to catch God's blessings, it will not be long before passers-by can take shelter under the shadows of our wide-spread oaks of thankfulness.

We have to learn to be thankful; we are selfish by nature. We must not and cannot take blessings and favors as a matter of course. We have done nothing to merit them, so why should we receive them as if they were rightfully ours. We owe God everything. He owes us nothing. He has given us life, and instead of being thankful for every breath we draw, we murmur and complain that we were not born in a different place or at a different time or in different circumstances. We complain because we have trials, we suffer pain, we must shed tears of sorrow, have disappointments and lose friends. We often grieve Him by wishing we had never been given life at all. Get all you can out of life! Live! Be glad you are alive, and make yourself a part of life and God. Let your life be one of thanksgiving and show it at every opportunity.

What if we do have misfortunes? Are they any greater than those of a hundred thousand other people? Maybe we don't understand why they happen to us. Job didn't understand his misfortunes either; but he never gave way to ingratitude. He must have had the hardest blow of all when his wife wouldn't stand by him. We, like Job's wife, sometimes would like to strike out at God when our loved ones are stricken with illness. We must remember that God is no respector of persons and that many of God's greatest servants suffered severely, even Christ.

Sometimes our suffering is for a purpose. Men have been brought to their knees before God through suffering. God will give us strength to bear it, for which we must be thankful. God will never fail us nor forsake us. If we ask in faith, He will answer our prayers. We must remember, though, to always pray, "Thy will be done," for fear of asking for something that would make us worse off. "Ask, and it shall be given you, seek, and ye shall find; knock, and it shall be opened unto you" (Matthew 7:7). But be ready to receive with glad hearts and thanksgiving or you might find yourself with the "Oh, ye of little faith."

I Am Thankful!

"I sat in a hospital room the other day where dozens of others were waiting and saw countless numbers of little babies stricken with a dreadful disease, and I was thankful for the great years that I have enjoyed my children in their good health.

"I see so many broken homes and homeless children and then remember the Christian father and mother and all the brothers and sisters that I have who are faithful Christians themselves, and I am thankful.

"I see and hear of churches over the brotherhood that are torn asunder with troubles of all kinds and then I think of our pleasant work with the church here at home, and I am thankful.

"I look around me in the world and see people who are not free and then I look at those of us in America, and then I am thankful.

"I see millions still groping in the world of sin, without God and without hope in the world to come, and then I think of the Son of God who gave Himself that I might be redeemed, and I am thankful.

"I hear of the millions in other parts of the world who will literally starve to death in the years to come, and then I think of the tables at which we feast, and I am thankful.

"I think of those who have nothing to look forward to after this life is over, and then I remember the blessings too numerous to mention which my Father will give me after death, and I am thankful.

"Why don't you stop to count your blessings? If you will, then you will be thankful that you have so many blessings to count."

Ted Knight
Middletown Church of Christ
Middletown, Rhode Island

For several years my husband and I prayed fervently for a child. With feelings of doubt and self-pity, I would think, "Does God hear us when we pray?" After 13 years we were able to adopt a beautiful baby girl. How good God is! Our daughter has been and still is such a comfort to me. When she was 12 years old my husband died of a massive heart attack. Soon to follow was my own illness of acute diabetes and rheumatoid arthritis. But my daughter's good influence and Christian attitude would then become my mainstay. Many were the times when I felt I must stay home from worship on the Lord's Day or from the mid-week services, but she would invariably say, "Shouldn't we start getting ready for worship?"

"In the day of prosperity be joyful, and in the day of adversity consider; God has made the one as well as the other. . . ." (Ecclesiastes 7:14 RSV).

The ungrateful heart is a sick heart. It is even sicker than the heart that had the massive attack, for it is self-centered and selfish. It is a heart that feels that life owes it everything and that it should do nothing in return. A heart such as this fails even to recognize blessings from God, much less be grateful for them.

When you go to the supermarket, are you thankful that you are able to go or do you complain about the prices?

Do you ever think to tell that special friend that you are glad she is your friend, or do you feel that she is the one who should feel grateful?

Do you think to tell your husband every day that you are grateful to God for him, or do you start his day with complaints?

Do you ever tell your children how proud you are of them? Most of us are quick to tell them of their misdeeds but don't often tell them of all the right things they do.

Most important of all—how long has it been since you told God how thankful you are that He is always near, or do you have to be struck down to remember to tell Him?

The Deacon's Thanksgiving

Old Deacon Bedell was the cheeriest man
You'd meet within many a day;
He 'lowed that the Lord had a pretty good plan
For running the world, and he'd say
I'm thankful that things are about as they are—
They could be a mighty sight wuss
And the things we've complained of the loudest so far
Have proved to be blessings to us.
When others lamented the drought, he'd reply
It's better than havin' a flood,
And we ought to thank God when the weather is dry,
That we don't have to waller in mud!
Yet, when it was stormy he'd never complain,
But say with immutable trust;
The Lord in his goodness has sent us the rain
To lay this discomfortin' dust.
When adversity smote him, it fell like the dew,
On mountains impervious crest,
For his simple philosophy held to the view
That everything worked for the best.
And for others misfortunes he always could find
Such sweet consolation to give,
It seemed that he envied the halt and the blind
The lives they were destined to live.
One day he was caught in a threshing machine;
It cost him a leg, but he said;
That's getting off cheaper than some I have seen,
I'm thankful it wasn't my head."
And always thereafter he stumped on a peg,
Or patiently went with a crutch
Declarin', I'm saving a lot on that leg—
My socks only cost half as much!
When his end was approaching, he said with a smile,

As they folded his hands on his breast;
I've worked pretty hard for a considerable while,
And I'm thankful to get a good rest.
He went through the world strewing smiles on his way,
And neighbors surviving him tell
That no matter what happened, it seemed every day
Was Thanksgiving to Ezra Bedell.

—Arthur W. Hawkins

Gratitude and appreciation for one's blessings seem to come, then, not to those who have the best material surroundings but to those who have learned how to master this blessed and peaceful state of thankfulness. Riches can be a handicap. A wealthy woman told her doctor she was frustrated by a restless desire for more and more things. He replied, "These are the usual symptoms of too much ease in the home and too little gratitude in the heart." In Deuteronomy 8:10-11 we read, "When thou . . . . art full, . . . beware that thou forget not the Lord."

Somewhere—

—a mother is trying to make up her mind whether to let a surgeon do an operation on her only son, that may take his life.
—a man, whose son didn't come home last night, is walking through a door marked, "City Morgue."
—a wife, whose marriage has "gone on the rocks," is on the street corner flirting with a man she knows will destroy her fidelity.
—a man is sitting on his bed toying with a pistol, while his wife is shrieking at him from the bottom of the stairs to come down and explain his recent whereabouts.
—a young woman is being wheeled into the delivery room from which she knows that mother or child (not mother and child), will be wheeled out.
—a tired doctor is shaking his head and saying, "Terminal cancer."
—a woman is wondering how she is going to tell her son that she knows he is the criminal the police are looking for.
And Somewhere—

—a contented "Christian" decides to stay home from the worship of the Lord because he has nothing in particular for which to be thankful.

Mrs. Bess Stewart
1129 Mt. Vernon Road
Memphis, Tennessee 38111

WHAT PRICE
—CHILDREN?

From the subject of this chapter one might assume that we are going to talk about the rearing of children from a negative view—that is, in terms of dollars and cents. However, I prefer to take a more positive approach and show that the assets of rearing children far outweigh the liabilities. A baby is born into this world in total innocence and has the potential of becoming a great citizen, depending on how the parents nurture and train it through the years that lie ahead.

The wise man, Solomon, said, "Train up a child in the way he should go: and when he is old, he will not depart from it" (Proverbs 22:6). From this truth we can deduce that there is a right way and also a wrong way to train up a child. Observation and experience have convinced me that there are good Christian parents who want to rear their children in the nurture and admonition of the Lord but for some reason are complete failures. Samuel was a man of God, but could not control the evil conduct of his sons. He made them judges over Israel, but they turned after lucre, took bribes and perverted judgment. Eli, a priest of God and closely associated with Samuel, also had sons; however, in 1 Samuel 3:13 it is said that "Eli's sons made themselves vile, and he restrained them not." It would appear that Samuel was concerned about the conduct of his sons, but that Eli was not concerned about the conduct of his sons and was therefore condemned.

Although I know of no magic formula that will always work in the rearing of children, the scriptures indicate that parental love and proper discipline are essential. "He that spareth his rod hateth his son: but he that loveth him chasteneth him betimes" (Proverbs 13:24). "Withhold not correction from the child: for if thou beatest him with the rod, he

59

shall not die" (Proverbs 23:13). "And, ye fathers, provoke not your children to wrath: but bring them up in the nurture and admonition of the Lord" (Ephesians 6:4). Discipline should be administered for the right reason, to demonstrate the difference between right and wrong behavior. In the process of disciplining their children, many parents only provoke them to wrath. The discipline which is applied is not from a spirit of love. As a result, children become resentful, fail to respect their parents' authority and sometimes even leave home.

Knowing that my parents loved me had an abiding influence on my life. When I was about 10 years old, I overheard two of my aunts talking about my father and how much he loved his children. I knew he did, but I was glad to hear it affirmed by someone else's observation.

At the early age of 4 I was deeply impressed with an incident that happened in our neighborhood. A young teenage boy who was constantly causing trouble finally did something serious enough to land him in jail. When his mother went to see him he said, "Why didn't you make me do right? If you had made me do right, I would not be in this jail." Perhaps he was right, but the thought that comes to my mind in this true story is that trying to *make* children do right is entirely the wrong approach. We are to influence our children to do right by precept and example.

Timothy's great faith was developed because of the example of faith in the lives of his mother and grandmother, 2 Timothy 1:5. Children should not be made to attend Bible classes and worship services, for they should follow their parents there as a matter of course. One of the greatest gifts we can bestow upon our children is a good example. Oliver Goldsmith once said, "A child seldom improves when he has no model but himself to follow."

When speaking of the education of children, most people think in terms of the "three R's." Education is thought of as a purely academic process brought about in a formal teaching situation. However, education involves much more; it is a continuing process that begins with life itself. It is any type of learning whether good or bad, and it can be physical, mental, social or spiritual. It is the responsibility of all parents to see to it that their children receive the proper kinds of education. Many parents are more concerned about educating children as to how to make a living to the neglect of teaching them how to live. Most leading educators who have attempted to define education have completely ignored religious or Christian education, which is actually the most important and most enduring.

We can look to no greater example than the education of the Lord Jesus Christ. When He was 12 years of age we read that He "increased in wisdom and stature, and in favour with God and man" (Luke 2:52). It may be more costly financially to educate in all categories in which our Lord was educated, but the investment pays large dividends in the way of joy, happiness and pride. Let us examine in more detail the way in which Jesus was educated.

Wisdom. Knowledge is the acquisition of information about anything in any phase of education. Wisdom is training in how best to apply knowledge to the greatest benefit. We send our children to school to acquire not only knowledge of but wisdom in the use of English, math, geography, history, etc. Growing in wisdom is learning to do anything better. Jesus was growing in wisdom when He was being tutored by his father to be a good carpenter. He was growing in wisdom of geography when He walked up and down the hills from Jerusalem to Galilee.

Stature. To state that Jesus grew in stature indicated that He did those things that caused his physical body to be strong. The physical development of our bodies is important because our souls dwell within. Paul said in 1 Corinthians 3:16, "Know ye not that ye are the temple of God, and that the Spirit of God dwelleth in you?"

In favor with God. Above all else in the education of our children, we should train them to live in favor with God, for then all other phases of education will naturally fall in line. It is natural for us to desire God's favor and blessing. Abraham prayed that he might have favor in the sight of God and he received favor. But receiving God's favor requires effort on our part. Paul taught that we must "Study to shew thyself approved unto God, a workman that needeth not to be ashamed, rightly dividing the word of truth" (2 Timothy 2:15).

In favor with man. Most people feel the necessity of living in favor with God, but many do not consider it important to strive to live in favor with men. Paul stated in Romans 12:18, "if it be possible, as much as lieth in you, live peaceably with all men." We read in 1 Peter 2:9 that God's people are to be a peculiar people. In this setting some feel that Peter is teaching that Christians are queer and contentious so as to be disliked by people of this world. On the contrary, it simply means that Christians are to be a unique and distinctive people. They are to so conduct their lives that they will find favor with their fellow men and, therefore, influence them for good. Jesus said, "Let your light so shine before men, that they may see your good works and glorify your Father which is in heaven. (Matthew 5:16). In giving the qualifications for elders, Paul stated that "He must have a good report of them which are without"(1 Timothy 3:7). He means that an elder should be well thought of in the community. Our children should also be taught to live peaceably with other children so long as they can do so without sacrificing truth.

There are three possible sources of Christian education—the home, the church and the Christian school. We cannot over-emphasize the importance of Christian education in the home. Daily Bible study and prayer should be a habit in every home. However, the day-to-day example of godly living set by parents is the best teacher. The atmosphere of the home should reflect the spirit of Christ.

Faithful attendance to Bible classes and the worship services of the church is a vital and necessary part of a child's spiritual training. The teaching received from dedicated Christian teachers and preachers will complement and reinforce the teaching received in the home. The services of the church are designed to build up and strengthen Christians. This in turn will strengthen the family if all will attend.

Finally, I would strongly suggest the advantages of sending children to Christian schools. Christian schools offer the advantage of exposing children to a Christian atmosphere whether they are in a chemistry class or playing basketball. They offer the advantage of daily Bible classes and chapel programs under the leadership and teaching of dedicated and scholarly Bible teachers. Christian education is expensive when thought of in terms of dollars and cents; but consider the fact that 90% of our Christian young people who attend state institutions of higher learning leave the church. What price can we place on the value of the soul?

Our Christian colleges have for years been jokingly referred to as "matrimonial institutions." In my opinion this is a great compliment. Young Christian men and women are brought together in social relationships where they can learn to know each other better and choose a life's companion. They are given a good foundation upon which to build for the future. What an enormous dividend!

Much has been written in recent years about the increasing financial problems of private colleges. I cannot believe that the thousands of

Christians in the United States will ever allow our Christian schools to be forced to close their doors. What a tremendous price we would pay if we were to abandon our full programs of Christian education. Just so long as we support our private Christian schools can we be assured of a more adequate supply of Gospel preachers, elders, deacons, Bible teachers, Christian fathers and mothers.

What price children?

Mr. Rufus G. Hibbett
637 North Cherry
Florence, Alabama

A CHILD
OF
THE HEART

God must have known what extra joy and how extra testing would enhance our lives through the care of orphans. There are so many scriptures that tell of great blessings for those who help others— Matthew 25:40, Acts 20:35, 2 Corinthians 9:9, etc. In James 1:27 we find a very definite command to care for orphans: "Pure religion and undefiled before God and the Father is this, To visit the fatherless and widows in their affliction, and to keep himself unspotted from the world."

At the time when many were arguing the *method* of caring for orphans, my husband and I decided one thing for sure—that no matter *how* we did it, we must *do* it! The churches we were working with were being supported by others; therefore, none of our contribution was going to orphans. We felt that the only way we could do our duty was by using our home. We were living in a new three-bedroom house and only had one son, age 1, at the time. We decided to *do* it and left it with the Lord.

We didn't seem to wonder if we could "find room in our hearts" or if "blood was really thicker than water," we mainly just accepted it as one of God's commands with promise. It is strange to us that more people do not see it as a command to *them* at all.

The purpose of our "adoptions," then, was three-fold: to save, to be saved and to be a light to others so that God would be glorified (Matthew 5:16).

Since adopting two children and having two of ours by birth, I must admit that the concept of "adoption" has been greatly enlarged in my mind. In my own mind, as in most other people's, I pictured a sweet, innocent babe being taken into the loving arms of a couple who had waited years for the opportunity of rearing a child, giving it many good things in life. This child naturally would turn out to be a beautiful, graceful and charming person with hardly a problem!

We were working at a Christian camp one summer, and since it was a six-week camp we became very close to the campers. We had met Richard (then age 13) the summer before and knew that he lived with his paternal grandmother, who was well advanced in age.

One day he told us that he didn't know what he would do, because his grandmother had been injured on her job and could not support them any longer. His older brothers were already living in a "welfare" home, and it looked very possible that he would be placed in one also. He was so worried that the joy of camp was gone for him. At night when we knew he must have been awake thinking of his future, we were also thinking and praying.

After camp we took Richard home and met his grandmother and explained our wish to help. She agreed it would probably be best for Richard to come live with us. While we were there talking, both of us realized that this was the opportunity for which we had prayed.

Richard visited his grandmother every summer for a couple of weeks, and she came to see us each year until she died. She was a Christian who did "all she could."

Richard went into the army after high school and did very well; we even had a letter from his commanding officer saying what a fine man he was. Richard is now an executive in a well-known company, but best of all he is a member of the Lord's church. Richard was and is still today a great blessing to us, along with our daughter-in-law and grandson.

In time God blessed us with a beautiful baby girl—the first granddaughter in my husband's family in 14 years! What more could we ask? She loved and was loved by her two older brothers. Our home was full of love, discipline and peace. Our children were well-behaved, socially adjusted and maturing Christians. We had no "generation gap."

When talking with friends about the possibility and need of helping another child, they would say, "You've done enough," or "You owe it to Sue, Richard and Peter (our first-born) to give them more time and attention and things.''

Richard was married, Peter was going off to college and we again realized that we would have an empty room. We wanted our daughter to always feel special, yet not grow selfish by not having anyone with whom to share. We felt that our experience with Richard had been such a good one that we would try again. We talked with our children, and they, too, were eager to try. Almost a year passed; then one of our friends told us about Brian.

Brian was 10 years old, adoptable, and in a treatment center in the big city near us. This center was for emotionally disturbed children. It wasn't exactly what we had in mind, but the very idea of a child in desperate need touched our hearts. We called to make an appointment. We still had many doubts. We prayed, we discussed, we went.

His social worker, Mrs. Overstreet, had had 18 years experience in this work and was very methodical, not stern, yet pretty formidable. She quickly informed us that in the 100-year history of "the home," only one child had been legally adopted. All the other children had at least one parent who wouldn't let them go, but not Brian—he had no one.

She gave us forms and told us to each write an autobiography, get a physical exam, three references, etc. She showed us a picture of Brian. I'll never forget her remark after we were so pleased over his picture. "Looks like a real all-American boy, doesn't he?" Then she began to tell us about his history. The only thing I could remember in his favor was that he was pretty healthy *now*. He had been malnourished upon arrival at the home. He had been in eight foster homes and two institutions between the ages of 2 and 10 and each change had caused him to feel more and more rejected and worthless.

Mrs. Overstreet said it took her three months to get him to come into her office and sit down to talk. He would just stand at her door during her interviews with him. At this center there were many qualified people to work with the children. They agreed that Brian was the hardest "case" they had encountered.

He became silent and morose; he began to hurt others, mostly small children and animals; he began to steal and lie and set fires. At school Brian was a poor student and spent most of his time in the office of the principal because of discipline problems.

They told us Brian trusted no one. Every adult (in his mind) had let him down, and he had been replaced by a smaller child everywhere he had been. These things were basically true. We could see how he could have these feelings and behavior problems, but we wondered if we could possibly do for him what so many others had not been able to do.

Mrs. Overstreet told us we could not expect to even see Brian for weeks but after talking about an hour with us, she said, "His school bus will be here shortly and I'll point him out to you, but you will not be able to talk with him." When the bus came, we walked outside and she pointed him out. I was shocked at how thin and poor he looked. He had a stocking cap pulled down almost over his eyes, and he didn't look anything like the boy in the picture. It was cold, and he had his hands in his pockets and was not laughing or playing with the others. (There were 39 children in the "center" at the time.) He was walking to the building with his head down.

Mrs. Overstreet suddenly called to him and said (to our astonishment), "Brian, this is Mr. and Mrs. Jones, and they are interested in adopting you!" She later told us that all her years of experience had taught her to follow her instincts, and she suddenly knew we should have Brian.

Things kept moving very quickly, and in two weeks Brian was at our house for the weekend. It was the beginning of a series of traumatic experiences for the formerly peaceful Jones family, I can tell you!

We knew that Brian was interested in insects, so we took a nice new insect book with us when we picked him up for the first visit. He promptly lost it. On the way to our house (an hour's drive) we learned that he hated being cooped up, couldn't sit still and asked silly questions (on purpose, continuously) to cover his nervousness. We also learned that he smelled like an outdor john! On the trip he asked me to fill in the identity card for his new billfold. (It was new because he had just stolen it that day!)

We started losing "friends" quickly after Brian's arrival. It was easy to understand. In fact, he was the very type child we had kept our children away from! He had a filthy mouth at age 10! We learned things the like of which we had never heard. If and when Brian would shake hands with an adult, he would grab their thumb and hang on for dear life! He could stare down the bravest.

At the table Brian resembled a cave man eating (before he devised utensils). The noises he emitted must also have been similar. He only liked certain foods and made loud derogatory remarks about anything else. He never let go of his glass; he would chomp, then gulp, till everything was gone. We prayed constantly for wisdom and patience.

We stopped having our usual amount of company and only had the bravest and truest of our friends visit us. Our invitations dropped to the above mentioned. Our daughter was in "shock." Other girls (who didn't know Brian) said, "Oh, all kid brothers are the same!" She could get no sympathy. We were trying so hard to show Brian the same considerations that we did Sue; but, thank goodness, we were led to a wonderful Christian psychologist who told us to quit trying to treat them the same, that it wasn't possible. Believe me, we were convinced!

Mrs. Overstreet was a constant help. For over a year she called every week, and I called her for advice and counseling. Many times we thought we couldn't take it any longer. We had all decided, however, that with the Lord's help we would not turn back. Brian would be our very own someday. Sometimes the very thought would make us weep—and not tears of joy!

Brian had to be watched constantly; he never seemed to rest. My husband and I took turns. We never asked Sue to join in this, for we didn't want to hear her refuse. Actually, he was not her responsibility. She was never unkind to him. She never asked him to do anything or to stop doing something. In fact, she just couldn't bear to talk to him anymore than necessary. By this time she had already been the one who had saved the neighbor child from having his eyes "torn out" by Brian. Brian had chopped the end of her cat's tail off, poked one puppy down our drain (it died from injuries), played catch with another. She knew there was nothing good she could say. We didn't force her. We knew we were having many similar feelings.

There was the night we took Brian to the basketball game and unwittingly allowed him to go purchase some popcorn. We knew better, but every now and then we'd tell ourselves, "He is 11 years old; surely he can do this!" He stayed and stayed until we were about to go after him. We were sitting in the back of the balcony. Suddenly we heard the bass drum behind the curtains on the stage of the gymnasium. The basketball game was going strong. The principal (a friend of ours) appeared and hastened toward the stage. He reappeared with a young boy leading the way who broke loose and ran all the way around the gymnasium. Yes, it was Brian.

Brian loved sports, and he was good at anything he tried. He had one problem—he never heard the word, "teamwork." If someone accidentally bumped him, he gave them a black eye. He was using the skateboard at school and a boy bumped him. Brian promptly gathered speed and made a direct hit! He didn't care if he did have to have four stitches—the other boy had to have eight! The coach tried to be his friend and to help him; Brian helped himself to the coach's stop watch!

When it became necessary for me to have surgery, we had a problem. Who would "watch" Brian? All baby sitters (grown people, of course) had been turning us down. We called my husband's mother. She was delighted. She had been wanting a chance to help with Brian. After six boys of her own, she just knew she would have no problem with him. He criticized her cooking; he wet the bed every night and soiled his pants every day; he said, "Oh yeah, so what!" and wouldn't mind her. Then one day the neighbor called and said, "Come get this child!" Brian had stabbed his dog with our ice pick (which we kept carefully hidden) and had then cursed our neighbor. The dog lived, but the vet asked, "How is the child?" It had not attacked Brian!

Grandmother now prays with us often and has a very sympathetic ear, because since that visit Brian has let her chickens out several times, stolen from her grocer, killed her favorite butterfly and tromped her flowers.

Our older son was sure he could relate to him since he was adopted also. He took him for one weekend. He confessed that he was wanting to spank him 15 minutes after he took him. Brian had threatened the life of his child! He had also caused his own nose to bleed, and Richard became so frightened that he brought him back early. Unknown to Richard, Brian brought a snake home with him in his clothes sack. Richard now prays for us earnestly also.

Speaking of snakes reminds me of the day one of our last (fast-fading) friends had volunteered to have Brian for a few hours. He had walked into her kitchen where she was cooking supper with a five-foot long black snake hanging around his neck! She didn't help us with Brian again for a long time. She, too, is praying.

Many times I regretted having sacrificed my precious free time and the hours that Sue and I could have had gadding about shopping or visiting together. Every moment and all energy seemed to be centered on Brian. "Is it worth it? Are we helping Brian at all?' we asked ourselves. People began to say, "Oh, he's changed so much! Don't give up, he's improving."

I'll never forget the day, after two years, when our daughter yelled at Brian. I was so happy that I had to leave the room. She had reacted normally to her mean little brother! Brian was so shocked that he listened to her. Littly by little we were all progressing.

We learned that Brian could play with others for almost an hour at a time now without a calamity. He could remain in a classroom for almost the entire time without being sent out. We could eat a meal with him without losing our appetites. He smelled so much better (although he still wets the bed nightly). He seldom steals now, although Sue's senior ring suddenly disappeared recently. His language is much improved—at least in public. Brian smiles more now.

Brian had been sprinkled in the Catholic church. When he came to us we began intensive Bible training. He learned quickly. He also found that many in his Bible classes were *not* studying at all and that he had all the answers. He enjoyed this success tremendously. We also emphasized that God loves each of us and that if we do his will *He* will *never* leave us or forsake us. This appealed to Brian because he had been forsaken by so many. He also actually had a very low opinion of himself, although outwardly he made a constant show of egotism. He began to want to be more like others and to be liked by them.

When he was 12, Brian was baptized. He knew many scriptures by this time and had even given a talk on "love" to our congregation. We stressed that repentance was necessary, which also meant he had to make many changes.

We still have a lot of mountains to climb with him, and people ask, "Would you do it again, knowing what you know now?" My answer is that many of us would never have children at all if we could see all the trials and problems beforehand.

Brian and Richard are "children of the heart" and are very special to us. Our prayer is that we can all enter "together" on that great day. It will be worth it all!

In any large city near you there are many "hard to place" children just waiting for your love and help. As stated, most of these children are not up for adoption or even able to stay in permanent foster homes. There is a need for weekend homes, holiday homes, people to take them to the doctor or dentist. Older people are needed as "aunts, uncles and grandparents" for them.

These children are from 8 to 14 years old and already have many problems that can seldom be entirely solved. On the other hand, these children are each potentially a child of God, or a dependent citizen who will probably grow up to be harmful or useless. One of these "special ones" could save your soul.

Editor's Note: For obvious reasons the writer of this chapter prefers to remain anonymous. All names used are fictitious.

UNEQUALLY
YOKED
TOGETHER

This chapter is written to encourage those Christians who have an unbeliever as a partner in marriage. Parents and religious leaders have traditionally objected to the marriage of Christians and non-Christians; however the Lord does not forbid such marriages.

If any brother hath a wife that believeth not, and she be pleased to dwell with him let him not put her away. And the woman which hath an husband that believeth not, and if he be pleased to dwell with her, let her not leave him. For the unbelieving husband is sanctified by the wife, and the unbelieving wife is sanctified by the husband: else were your children unclean: but now they are holy. But if the unbelieving depart, let him depart. A brother or a sister is not under bondage in such cases: but God hath called us to peace. For what knowest thou, O wife, whether thou shalt save thy husband? or how knowest thou, O man, whether thou shalt save thy wife (1 Corinthians 7:12-16).

Usually the reason for objection to such marriages is the hardship placed on the partners involved. All married couples have problems; but in a marriage between partners of different religious backgrounds the number of problems is increased, and some problems that would normally exist are magnified. To achieve happiness, each individual must possess above average understanding and tolerance.

In this day and age when divorce seems to be the way out for so many, Christians know that this is not God's plan. Every effort must be made to make a success of marriage. Under the best of circumstances you can expect to have stress in your marriage. If we find ourselves in the situation of being married to an unbeliever, we should and must do everything possible to win him/her to Christ so that we can know what joy and peace and happiness can be with God's Word as the mediator in all our difficulties. If this is not possible then the Christian partner must use God's Word for his/her guide and the marriage can be improved every day. "Cast thy burden upon the Lord, and he shall sustain thee: he shall never suffer the righteous to be moved" (Psalms 55:22).

Typical symptoms of marital discord are difficulties over spending the family income, in-laws, sex relations, social activities and friends, personality conflicts and religious life. God's Word holds many answers for you concerning each of these difficulties.

Giving as we have been prospered is a command of the Lord, and obedience to this command is one of the ways we show our love for Him (1 Corinthians 16:2). Difficulties regarding giving may arise if the partner who is the wage earner is the partner who is not a Christian.

It would be unusual if questions about money did not play an important part in married life. Most of a wage earner's working period is devoted to earning it, and much of the rest of his time is devoted to spending it or making use of things that money has bought. You can readily see his reluctance to "give his money away." Try working out a budget where the Christian receives an allowance that can be spent as he/she desires. Or it may be that the Christian partner could earn extra money by making a hobby a part-time business. Never neglect obedience to God's commands to gain respect of the unbelieving partner, for each time you do, you lose some self-respect.

Husbands and wives from different religious backgrounds may also face rejection by in-laws, or even by their own parents and relatives. For this reason it is not wise to seek help or advice from relations. Establishing a good marriage becomes even harder because you will have to make it for yourselves. If there is any change in your relationship, you must be the instigator of this change. Do not let in-laws or relations criticize your relationship in your presence. As long as you live in this relationship, stand up for it.

Ephesians 5:28 says, "He that loveth his wife loveth himself." This is true also of a wife who loves her husband. You will not listen to criticism of someone you love. It is sometimes impossible to love the *conduct* of a person who reviles you and who violates the laws of

God. Yet, you may still love the *person*; we may speak kindly of him and to him. We should never treat our mate in such a way that we cannot pray for God's assistance in that treatment. God knew these problems would arise and gave us the answers in His Word: "For this cause shall a man leave father and mother, and shall cleave to his wife: and they twain shall be one flesh" (Matthew 19:5).

True marriage makes no provision for coldness. It is the duty and direct commandment of God to satisfy our mate's sexual desires. Our religious differences can never come between us and the fulfillment of a complete sexual life. If you will always remember this, you may avoid unfaithfulness in the unbelieving partner who may not feel infidelity is a sin. "The wife hath not power of her own body, but the husband: and likewise also the husband hath not power of his own body, but the wife" (1 Corinthians 7:4).

Simple, wonderful things like having close friends and socializing with them can cause problems in your marriage. The unbelieving partner may choose friends of this world, and to be a part of his world you must associate with them often. These contacts can involve drinking, gambling, filthy language and other things that make your heart ache. You cannot stay away from these friends because you would build yet another wall between you and your mate. You can remember that the example you set in their midst may lead someone to Christ. Your mate is aware of your example as a Christian whether he ever says so or not. Even Jesus had to mix and mingle with the world, not to condemn it; but that the world through Him might be saved (John 3:17).

Make for yourself Christian friends and spend some time with them so that your common goal—serving the Lord—can encourage and uplift you daily. If your mate will not share these friends, find time for them that will not inconvenience your marriage in any way.

Personality conflicts can be a source of trouble in your marriage. Rarely do marital disturbances result from the behavior of one partner alone but from the reactions of each partner to the other's actions. Your partner may have many of the things the Lord hates as a part of his personality. Your reaction to these traits will show him/her every day what a Christian is.

It is probably the rare husband or wife who is never susceptible to the pangs of jealousy. We usually think immediately of a person of the opposite sex when we think of this word. I would like to suggest that it is quite possible that if you are the Christian you should be, your spouse may be jealous of the Lord and His Church. When a husband or wife expresses displeasure at something so commonplace as Sunday worship, it may be that he/she is not confident of his mate's love. There may be no reason for this jealousy, but it is a genuine and disturbing threat nonetheless. Where he often errs is in thinking that he can remedy the situation by not attending worship and making it miserable for his partner to do so.

To overcome a persistent feeling of jealousy, there must be the development of enough self-esteem so that the individual can view his partner's relationship with the Lord in a more realistic fashion. This is easier said than done and you will have to help. Help consists mainly in relating to the feelings of personal inadequacy upon which this jealousy feeds. Husbands and wives who reach a stage of serious disruption almost always have little understanding of each other and little sympathy for each other's problems.

Personality differences may frequently give rise to anger. The venting of anger—blowing your top—rarely produces constructive results. You may say things in anger that you will always regret. Recognizing your own feelings of anger can be helpful in learning to control them. Anger almost always is our response to a real or imagined blow at our self-esteem. An angry response of your mate to a statement you have made likewise indicates that you have hurt his self-esteem in some way. If you can reconstruct the conversation, you can often uncover some traits in your partner's personality which will help in avoiding some future outburst of anger.

As the Christian partner you should be able to handle personality differences with a calm and loving spirit. Accept the fact that there are some things that you cannot change about your mate and be willing to forgive over and over the same personal blows. "For if ye forgive men their trespasses, your heavenly Father will also forgive you" (Matthew 6:14). ". . .forgive, and ye shall be forgiven" (Luke 6:37). "Let all bitterness, and wrath, and anger, and clamour, and evil speaking, be put away from you with all malice: and be ye kind one to another, tenderhearted, forgiving each other, even as God for Christ's sake hath forgiven you" (Ephesians 4:31-32).

The last source of marital difficulties we will discuss is probably the most difficult—religious life. If you are going to help your mate find the way to Christ, you must be the stronger of you two. You must stand firmly behind your desire to worship with the saints at every appointed time. Although frequent worship is one of your greatest avenues to learning more and to becoming a stronger Christian, your attendance should not become disruptive to your household.

Take for example the Christian wife who leaves for Sunday worship before her mate gets out of bed. Sunday is his only day off and his only day to sleep late. Getting the children ready and getting herself ready took all her time, and she did not have time to fix lunch. This means no breakfast and no lunch for a husband who does not understand why you have to go to worship anyway and especially doesn't understand why he has to sacrifice *his* day off for *your* religion. There is no need for this. It may be difficult, especially when your children are small, but you must plan ahead so that worship will just be a short time apart and not disrupt your house for the whole day.

The same holds true for your responsibilities as a Christian. No Christian can please God in a mere "dutiful" obedience to his commands. God wants a spiritual service, a free outpouring of our faith and love in all that we do. Plan for your visiting, teaching, and other duties to be done at a time that will not inconvenience your marriage. Your mate needs and deserves part of your life.

Many feel that the way to convert another person to Christ is through constant reminder of sin and the need for repentance. This approach may work outside of the marriage relationship, but in a marriage this could soon become constant nagging. Scripture warns us of this and gives us another way of teaching—by example. "It is better to dwell in the wilderness, than with a contentious and an angry woman" (Proverbs 21:19). ". . . be thou an example of the believers, in word. in conversations, in charity, in spirit, in faith, in purity" (1 Timothy 4:12). One of the best ways to get a reluctant spouse to worship and eventually to Jesus is to enable him to see how much it is benefiting you.

Do not be discouraged by other Christians who do not understand. I attended a personal work class at one time where the teacher made the statement that he did not see how anyone could go out and teach others if he could not teach the one person he loved most and came in contact with every day. I could have quit trying right then but I didn't. I still haven't converted my mate but it gives me a special joy to know that I have been instrumental in leading several others to Christ. There are those who just will not be converted. Some of Jesus' own family would not hear Him. Other Christians can never know your heart, only God in heaven. Don't give up!

Not listed as a typical symptom of marital discord but a great factor in family happiness is children. The Catholic Church will not recognize the marriage between a Catholic and someone of any other religious belief unless the person who is not a Catholic signs a paper saying their children will be brought up as Catholics. They also say if a child is taught Catholicism well until he is 7 he will always be a Catholic.

You should put at least this much or more emphasis on teaching your children Christianity. Jochebed taught Moses so well when he was little that all the riches and temptations in the court of Egypt could not sway him. Have a daily devotion with your children and maybe your partner will be reached through this. Don't just depend on this devotion but teach as the children of Israel were taught to teach their children. "And ye shall teach them your children, speaking of them when thou sittest in thine house, and when thou walkest by the way, when thou liest down, and when thou risest up. And thou shalt write them upon the door posts of thine house, and upon thy gates" (Deuteronomy 11:19-20).

Children must be taught from birth the importance of love and respect for both parents. Never use your unbelieving partner for a babysitter so that you can attend worship. This neglects the training of your child and gives the unbeliever an excuse for not going with you. As they grow older it may be that the children would rather stay home with the unbeliever and go fishing or help cook lunch than go to worship. If your children have already reached the teenage years, which are full of decisions, then your example is your greatest teaching tool just as it is with your mate.

If you and your mate can agree in private upon what is acceptable behavior for teenagers and stand together, then you already have half the battle won. However, acceptable behavior to the non-Christian is often unacceptable to a Christian. Unbelieving mothers can push teenage girls into the whirl of parties, dances, etc., that a Christian father would like to avoid. On the other hand a teenage boy will naturally pattern himself after his father whether the father is a Christian or not.

If you trained well in early childhood then God promises you that your child will come through these difficult years a better person. "Train up a child in the way he should go: and when he is old, he will not depart from it" (Proverbs 22:6). If not, then you will have to make every effort to convert your children just as you would any other unbelieving person, with love, patient teaching, example, and much prayer. An unknown author wrote: "The best way for a man to train up a child in the way he should go is to travel that way himself."

From this discussion you can see that the typical symptoms of marital discord are all problems that God in his infinite wisdom knew that we would have, and He has provided in his Word helps and solutions for all of these problems. Often I talk to someone who feels there is "no hope." This is a defeatist attitude and is found nowhere in the Christian heart. There is always hope and God's Word to encourage you.

The "no-hope" attitude comes from accepting one or more of the following false notions:

1. "Ignore the problem and it will go away." You cannot ignore the problem. If you have developed as a Christian then you should be becoming stronger every day. Instead of this making the problem smaller it will only intensify it. If you have not been growing stronger, then you are a weaker Christian and chances are guilt is eating away at you. This also will intensify the problem. A problem is a problem and cannot be solved by pretending it does not exist.

2. "All problems can be solved logically." Those who would consider a problem strictly on logical grounds generally ignore the part played by feelings and emotions, and our love for both our mate and our Lord involves both of these.

A purely rational approach also tends to consider a problem as it appears on the surface as being the whole problem. Of course this is rarely so. Your mate's failure to attend worship with you is not the problem but the reasons why your mate will not attend worship with you. When you are trying to convert someone to Christ you are sometimes trying to change the very attitude toward life which their parents taught them from birth. A rational person treats the symptoms while the cause of the trouble continues.

3. "You shouldn't feel the way you do." Despite what many persons believe, you cannot turn your feelings on and off at will. You may have been told that your problems could all be solved if you would compromise and both of you attend an entirely unrelated protestant denomination. This is impossible because you do "feel the way you do." As a Christian you know God's commands and know that obedience to these commands is necessary for your soul's salvation. For these reasons

you must feel the way you do, and if your mate cannot understand this you will have to adjust.

4. "I know what your real feelings are." It is the rare relationship that shares everything. You can never know another person's feelings. Regardless of how much you may disagree, or how far removed from your own experience it may be, your partner's point of view has something to recommend it. He may have arrived at it through a long, carefully pursued reasoning process, or it may be a purely emotional response; but it cannot be dismissed. You need not agree with it, of course, but if you relate to it with respect and seek to determine its basis, you will be better able to understand it. The more you are able to understand, the more you will be able to teach points of God's love that your partner needs in his life.

If you will never let any of these false notions creep into your marriage there will always be hope. Try to imagine living in your marriage without knowing our loving Father. Then compare this situation to your marriage if you are willing to submit your whole life to God's ways, knowing His Word holds the connecting link between man and woman in all marriage adjustment.

If you do not find all the answers you need by yourself, it is not necessary for you to make the awful choice between putting up with this disturbing situation or ending your marriage. You have a wider range of aids to get your marriage on the right track than has ever been available before. To take advantage of help in solving marital difficulties when it is not possible to do so on your own, first realize that it is not sign of weakness to admit that you have an unhappy relationship. Many persons still find it difficult to accept this idea and therefore carry on the tendency of previous generations to try to hide marital and family problems from public view. Denial of serious troubles will solve nothing. Difficulties should be brought out and dealt with.

We have already discussed disadvantages of seeking counsel from friends and relatives. There is another danger in seeking help from this source, and that is that your confidences may be exposed. Thus, you risk not only mutual embarrassment but also your mate's anger at having details of your private life exposed. You might begin by discussing your problems with an elder or your minister. Here you can feel more confident of receiving sympathetic consideration and of having your privacy respected. Also, these men have probably had experience with your very same problems before. Often we feel we are the only one with this or that problem when there are many "in the same boat."

If you do not feel that your problem is great enough to seek outside help, then there are many, many answers for you in Christianity. Your greatest source of help is your personal contact with God—PRAYER. He knows your every need even before you call on Him, and if you are obedient to His ways, He will grant what is best for you. "It shall come to pass, that before they call, I will answer; and while they are yet speaking, I will heal" (Isaiah 65:24).

Prayer without knowledge of the scriptures produces a religion without proper balance—zeal without wisdom. Bible study and prayer must be kept properly balanced. Keep in mind that if you have done everything you can to be a Christian inside your home as well as within the Lord's Church and your unbelieving partner breaks the bond of marriage and departs, there is no need for shame. God knew this could happen. "But if the unbelieving depart, let him depart. A brother or a sister is not under bondage in such cases: but God hath called us to peace" (1 Corinthians 7:15).

You can never relax in your attitude toward a strong and active Christian life. Put God first! You have an obligation to your mate, but he/she does not come first. There will be times in your marriage when your love for the Lord seems to be your only problem and when your mate will use this as a weapon against you. If this happens, Jesus offers comfort with these words: "Blessed are ye, when men shall revile you, and persecute you, and shall say all manner of evil against you falsely, for my sake. Rejoice, and be exceedingly glad: for great is your reward in heaven" (Matthew 5:11-12).

Even if we are in a difficult situation in our marriage and our personal family circumstance is not good, when we become Christians we become members of the greatest family ever. Enjoy this relationship to the fullest.

One of the most important characteristics of a Christian is the habit of happiness. "Rejoice always . . . for this is the will of God in Christ Jesus for you" (1 Thessalonians 5:16-18 RSV). "The fruit of the Spirit is love, joy, peace. . ." (Galatians 5:22). ". . .and your joy no man taketh from you" (John 16:22). Some people who are unhappy in their marriages would not be happy in any event. In order to be able to give happiness to others, it is necessary to have elements of a happy existence within oneself. Religion should contribute to personal happiness. The Christian has a basis for confidence in his own destiny. You cannot be blindly optimistic, for you know that life and society include evil and ugliness as well as goodness and beauty. But you can give others the benefit of the doubt, assuming that their motives and intentions are as generous as your own. This attitude contributes to your own happiness because you are not tormented by suspicions and distrustful doubts concerning your partner; it also contributes to the happiness of your mate by helping him to feel valued as an individual. "After all it is not what is around us, but what is in us; not what we have, but what we are, that makes us really happy" (Gelke). "Rejoice evermore . . . for this is the will of God in Christ Jesus concerning you" (1 Thessalonians 5:16-18).

For what knowest thou, O wife, whether thou shalt save thy husband? or how knowest thou, O man, whether thou shalt save thy wife? (1 Corinthians 7:16).

Note: The writer of this chapter prefers to remain anonymous.

THY WORKS
DO FOLLOW THEE

Erma Bombeck describes the years after 40 as the "in-between nap years." The children have left home and there is the tendency to feel useless. It is a time of self-evaluation and re-examination of the meaning of our lives. It is a time when we have to make choices. Prior to this period our lives have pretty much been planned for us. After the honeymoon is over a general pattern unfolds that most of us follow—the formula-mixing, diaper-washing years flow right into the mud-pie, sand box, lots of laundry years. From these we sort of fall into the teeth-straightening, piano-practicing, first date years; and finally with a firm hand and shaky knees we creep into the "I haven't a thing to wear" high school and college years. We wouldn't want to skip a single one of these years, and most of the time we thank God for them but it is the years that come next that we are going to concentrate on in this chapter—the "after 40" years.

It is extremely hard for any woman to try to devise a plan for another with any success. But there is a Master Plan which we can all follow and can be certain will work.

David, in Psalms 90:12, said for us to "number our days." In Proverbs 31:18 we read ". . .her candle goeth not out by night." A weary mother who has been up and down all night with a crying baby or sick child may not be able to "rise before dawn and reach forth her hands to the needy." The Lord knows this better than we. It is his plan that women be keepers at home, but there comes a time when we *can* reach out to help others—sharing a meal with a sick friend or needy family, a telephone call, a cheery visit to a shut-in, and the timely use of note pad and pen. A note of love to a sick friend or family who has suffered a loss can indeed bring a blanket of warmth to the shivering heart.

"What use is it, my brethren, if a man says he has faith, but he has no works? Can that faith save him? If a brother or sister is without clothing and in need of daily food, and one of you says to them, 'go in peace, be warmed and be filled,' and yet you do not give them what is necessary for their body, what use is that" (James 2:14-16 NASB).

". . .they may rest from their labors, for their deeds follow with them" (Revelation 14:13, NASB).

"Behold, I come quickly; and my reward is with me, to render to each man according as his work is" (Revelation 22:12 ASV).

The only Bible that the majority of people of this world ever read is the one lived in the lives of Christians. The love exemplified in our daily living does more toward preaching the Word and making our own salvation secure than a hundred sermons. Shakespeare said, "The evil that men do lives after them, the good is oft interred with their bones." His words may be true from a human standpoint but from God's view, which is the only one that counts, it is very false. Only the good that we do will help us reach our goal of a home in heaven.

We must realize our own powers and abilities whether they be in creative arts, leadership, athletic prowess, homemaking skills or in simply being a good listener. All too often a feeling of incompetence keeps us from venturing out into areas in which we don't feel secure. Where would our own Helen Keller have been if she had said, "I can't"? We insult God when we don't try to recognize the gifts He gives us. If we believe we are made in his image, we can't help but find strength. Until we let Him use his creative ability by letting it flow through us, we limit Him. Begin each day with the thought, "My time be in thy hand."

Now as never before in our society there is a problem that plagues us—loneliness. A recent poll revealed that 80% of the psychiatric patients interviewed stated that loneliness was the primary reason they sought help. Could it be that this feeling is brought about by too much preoccupation with self? A minister needed workers to sew for the handicapped. He went to a sanatorium to enlist the help of unoccupied patients. To his surprise there was a quick response to his request. Every patient there said, "NO!" They said, "We've got our own problems to worry about." It is easy to see why they were in this condition;—they had built walls instead of bridges into the lives of others. When we really learn to "rejoice with them that rejoice and weep with them that weep" we will soon forget about self.

Employment is the tonic of the mind, body and soul. An idle existence weakens the body; lack of exercise brings about a physical standstill. If we stand back and allow the cheeks of our friends and those in need of our help to become pale and their eyes lose their sparkle because of our own selfishness and indifference, our cheeks may lose their glow of health, our eyes their lustre, and our steps their elasticity and firmness. The mind becomes dulled with disuse—so, too, with the soul. Spiritual illness as well as physical illness is often caused by neglect and indifference.

I wouldn't say to the Lord in so many words, "Lord, I have so much to do today that I'm afraid to trust your management so I'll try to worry it out by myself." But my reluctance to believe His plan can order my day speaks louder than my formed words. We must become involved in service to others! We wouldn't hesitate to help when a crisis of some kind—blizzard, tornado, flood, etc.—strikes our area; yet daily we're in contact with people who are having inner crisis. The only way the world can know our Father is through His children. "You are the light of the world. Let your light shine before men in such a way that they may see your good works, and glorify your Father who is in heaven" (Matthew 5:14, 16 NASB). There is such a blessedness in giving. There is always someone poorer than ourselves who needs our kindness, or an encouraging word. Some lack temporal blessings that we may divide with them and do with a little less ourselves. How God's heart is gladdened and the giver's heart is enriched when silent alms are given. How beautiful benevolence is made by the everyday life of self-sacrifice and self-denial.

Don't hurry through life with a frown on your face,
And never a moment to spare
For the word and the smile are always worth while
In a world full of trouble and care.

There are others with burdens as heavy as yours,
Hearts weary with aching and pain,
That are longing to hear just a word of good cheer,
Will you let them be pleading in vain?

Don't feel that misfortune has singled you out
And made you her own special prey,
For you may be sure there's no home so secure
But that trouble will enter some way.

Anonymous

Do you remember the widow of Zarapheth to whom Elijah was directed? God said to Elijah, "I have commanded a widow woman there to sustain thee" (1 Kings 17:9). She had only a handful of meal and a little oil which she divided with Elijah, and neither the meal nor the oil failed—they multiplied. Not in the hoarding of them but in the spending she was blessed. When this stranger desired her to go and fetch some water to drink she readily went. She didn't object to the scarcity of it. The crucial test of what we believe is its effect on our daily living. Those around us may listen to every word when we express our beliefs, but in the end it's our actions that convince them.

It was such a miserably hot, humid day. The work was messy as the handful of men with paint rollers splattered paint on walls and ceiling. As one man wiped the paint from his face he commented, "We should do this more often!" What a strange remark under the circumstances. But they were enjoying the reward of painting the home of an elderly widow who was unable to do it. Jesus said, "But whosoever will be great among you, let him be your minister" (Matthew 20:26). We hold opportunities in our hands to sow so many deeds in Christ's name and bring enjoyment to other's lives. In our nation today one out of every eight persons will have some type of mental or emotional disorder. How can we bring happiness or comfort to these? There are mental health centers within our reach. We can show them we care by becoming volunteers and ministering unto their needs. The rewards will return unto us fourfold.

LINES FROM LIVING

I saw you standing there
    Along the way I live,
Your need was silently
    Asking me to give,
Perhaps of money pouch,
    Perhaps a loaf of bread,
Or of myself, my heart,
    Some helping hand, instead.
So finally you asked
    In verbal tone, and you
Received, for readily
    I gave what I could do.
But yet I know a feeling
    Of having done some wrong,

Since ask you must, my giving
Has waited far too long.

Martha Oliver Williams

"Bear ye one another's burdens, and so fulfil the law of Christ"
(Galatians 6:2). Perhaps you know a young widow with small children.
You can help with minor repairs around the house or with the children
for an afternoon so she can get out. Physical needs must be cared for
before they can be taught of God. We must show those around us that
we care before they can see that God cares.

LINES FROM LIVING

Your godliness
Lifts my drooping spirit.
Your serenity
In living for Him
Calms the restlessness
That claims my heart and soul.
You are many.
You are my Christian friend.

Martha Oliver Williams

Perhaps you can use the creative power God has given you by
performing a little magic in your kitchen. Sometimes it's hard to show
our care and concern for the lonely, sick or bereaved with words, but
preparation of a meal or special dish shows our care in a definite and
universally understood language.

Our world would be changed if each one lived a beautiful life each day.

WINDOWS

A beautiful life is made,
Not left to happenstance.
Each word of kindness,
Each thoughtful deed

Is painted into the work of art
Called living.

Martha Oliver Williams

"For the oppression of the poor, for the sighing of the needy, now will I arise" (Psalm 12:5). Are we afraid of becoming involved when there's a cry for help? If our ears are closed to the call of human needs, it is because our minds are empty of the knowledge of God. We know that God is mindful of us because we are made in His image, so we should in turn reach out to help our fellow man when he is in distress.

Recently, on an interstate highway, a car suddenly swerved off the pavement into an embankment. The car following quickly stopped and the driver ran to help. Only one man was in the wrecked car, and he was bleeding profusely. The concerned helper had fortunately been a medic and knew how to slow the bleeding while his wife flagged a passing motorist to call an ambulance. There was also the fear of an explosion. As it turned out, the man was taken to the hospital, the good Samaritans went back home to change clothing and made the meeting to which they were traveling but an hour late. Do we have time at the risk of our own life to save another? Is our conscience deadened, our hand shortened in reaching out to the needy because of fear, pride, racial prejudice, materialism, distrust and failure to respect God? Jesus tells us to ". . .come boldly unto the throne of grace, that we may obtain mercy, and find grace to help in time of need" (Hebrews 4:16).

We can observe some sterling traits in Onesiphorus of Ephesus who befriended Paul. Paul says, "He oft refreshed me." In the midst of overwhelming trials and imprisonment in Rome, Paul found himself revived when this humble and thoughtful Christian came his way. Onesiphorus wasn't afraid to associate himself with Paul's sufferings. As Paul says, "He wasn't ashamed of my chains." So many Christians today are harnessed with chains of sorrow and affliction. Do we shrink from helping them? Paul said, "He sought me out." He made it his business to find him. A minister advised a woman who felt useless to begin the next day to help someone during the morning and someone else at noon; then at night she should thank God for allowing her to help these two. She was asked to report back at the end of 10 days. Needless to say the suggestion had been a success—now she felt a sense of purpose. Great satisfaction comes from a purpose directed toward others and unassociated with self.

Seldom can a heart be lonely
If it seeks a lonelier still,
Self-forgetting, seeking
Only emptier cups to fill.

Our loneliness will evaporate when we start filling these emptier cups. In Acts 9 we find a picture painted for our example of a woman, Dorcas, filled with unbelievable sweetness. She showed her faith by her works and not merely words. What her hands found to do she did with all her might. Dorcas was first described as a disciple—a learner. What had she learned? By her every action she demonstrated a knowledge and understanding of Christ's words, "This is my commandment, That ye love one another, as I have loved you" (John 15:12). Dorcas probably realized she had but few talents from which to choose, but she did know that she had the gift of skillful hands. The gift she used right in her own home. No doubt early and late in the day she was making garments for widows and orphans of Joppa. What a renewed spirit they must have had to be wearing new and fitted garments instead of ill-fitting rags. We see their great love for her when at her death the widows stood by weeping and mourning their loss. They wept for themselves and their children who would soon find the want of such a good Christian. They asked Peter to have compassion on them and restore the one that has so fervently shown compassion to them. Those who are so charitable can ill be spared to die. She was indispensible! There were others raised from the dead but not because of their good works. What a joy it would be on the Day of Days if the angel would say of us, "She did her best for one of Thine." Dorcas was the epitome of the worthy woman in Proverbs 31. Almost 2000 years later Dorcas' name is synonymous with acts of charity because she gave so generously of herself to others.

We all know happy old couples who enjoy their later years together; but statistics point out the fact that women, in large numbers, outlive men. Unmarried women and widows dominate the feminine portion of our older generation. Not all of these women are able to live in their own homes or the homes of relatives. To be good stewards of our older years we need to think clearly and plan as concretely as possible for these years before they come. Especially should we develop attitudes and habits that will make us not only adaptable to other people, but able to draw on our own resources for the long hours we may have to spend alone. The best way to prepare for our winter years is to work hard during our springs and autumns, and the best way to work during these seasons is to always put the Lord first and others second. If this is practiced in all good faith in God's word, He *will* take care of us.

Then in that last great day may the King say to us, "Come, ye blessed of my Father, inherit the kingdom prepared for you from the foundation of the world: for I was an hungred, and ye gave me meat: I was thirsty, and ye gave me drink: I was a stranger, and ye took me in: naked, and ye clothed me: I was sick, and ye visited me: I was in prison, and ye came unto me" (Matthew 25:34-36). "Verily I say unto you, Inasmuch as ye have done it unto one of the least of these my brethren, ye have done it unto me" (Matthew 25:40).

Mrs. Sue Warmack
1902 Conway Drive
Florence, Alabama

THE BEST IS YET TO BE!

How do I begin writing about an experience I have not yet had—or about a person in whose moccasins I have not yet walked? Do I use my imagination, do I rely on ideas gathered through my own observation, or do I conduct personal interviews or borrow thoughts from others who have written concerning different phases of this subject? Although I have not reached what are considered (by reason of age) the latter years of my life, I have lived long enough to believe that "there is nothing new under the sun," and I realize that anything I write will be a reflection of something I have already seen, heard or read. So—with this in mind, I'd like to arrange a potpourri of thoughts which will hopefully be beneficial both to you, the reader, and to me.

Each of us is the product of a combination of different factors beyond our control—our place of birth, parents, race or color, early childhood experience, etc. However, regardless of our control over these circumstances we do begin to develop certain traits that manifest themselves very early in life and are usually accentuated as time goes on. A deeply-ingrained habit is hard to change, and I'm sure most of us can think of many habits we wish we had or had not formed when we were younger and easier to train. But once we have gotten into a path, we deepen it by continually traveling over it until eventually it is a gully so deep that getting out of it is difficult if not impossible.

Quite often we see older people who are self-centered, demanding, pessimistic and fault-finding; and we try to be generous in our excuse of them by saying they are old. Generally speaking, however, the truth is that these traits were present in their lives from the very beginning and instead of an effort at self-examination and correction, time has only made the unpleasant side of such people more obvious. We do not get this way overnight; it is a steady, continuous process in most cases. An exception, of course, would be for physical or mental reasons beyond our control. So attitudes play very important roles in the well-being and happiness of each of us, and although we sometimes have no control over our circumstances, we are able to control our attitude toward them. We should begin very early preparing for useful, productive and happy lives as senior citizens in the Lord's church. We can either be cheerful, happy and thoughtful of others or we can be bitter, unpleasant and miserable in our old age.

"Act the way you would like to be—and soon you will be the way you act."

Wouldn't it be great to be able to find the time to visit all those who need us—the shut-ins, the lonely, the bereaved and those who inspire us because of their example, youthful outlook and wisdom. But if we have not associated ourselves with them through the years there may be a real lack of understanding and appreciation on our part. It is not too early at any age to begin an association with older Christians; then if it is continued there is no generation gap about which we read so much these days. Several years ago one of the primary classes in our home congregation "adopted" a sweet little lady who was no longer able to come to the worship services. They mounted her picture on the bulletin board in their Sunday school room, talked about her service to the Lord, visited her and carried little gifts occasionally. I know that she was touched and pleased by their thoughtfulness, and I feel sure that it planted a seed in their hearts that keeps on growing. So many of our children today have little or no contact with the elderly, and it deprives both generations. Since our life of service is greatly influenced by the way we regard ourselves, we keep younger by being around young people. I wish more of our Bible school teachers would follow the example cited and help mold their pupil's respect and love for older people in the church. Here is an excellent recipe taken from my files. As there was no name attached, I regret that I cannot give proper credit.

How to Stay Young

YOUTH is not a time of life. . .it is a state of mind. **Nobody grows old by merely living a number of years; people grow old only by deserting their ideals. Years wrinkle the skin, but to give up enthusiasm wrinkles the soul. Worry, doubt, self-distrust, fear and despair. . .these are the long, long years that bow the head and turn the growing spirit back to dust. **Whether 70 or 16, there is in every being's heart the love of wonder, the sweet amazement at the stars and the starlike things—thoughts, the undaunted challenge of events, the unfailing childlike appetite for what next, and the joy and the game of life. **You are as young as your faith, as old as your doubt; as young as your self-confidence, as old as your fear; as young as your hope, as old as your despair.

With today's advancements in medical science the life span is increasing steadily. It is estimated that by the year 2000 (only a quarter of a century away) one in three Americans will be over 65. A society that has been concentrating on youth will necessarily become concerned with different priorities, and we need to be ready to keep pace in the church. Since so many opportunities for service already exist for our older Christians, their capabilities need to be harnessed and not allowed to rust. It is wonderful to see so many older women and men take advantage of Christian workshops and lectureships, to see them on campaigns and tours of Bible lands. Such experiences enrich their teaching abilities and deepen their appreciation of God's wonderful plan of salvation of *all* who obey and follow it.

"But," you say, "I can't leave home and go to all these places." You know, I once heard a woman in her 70's say that in all the years she had been a member of the church she had not been called on to do anything! Evidently she was content with this situation or else she would have attended all church activities and volunteered her services instead of being present only for the Sunday morning worship service. We are told to "Let your light so shine before men, that they may see your good works, and glorify your Father which is in heaven" (Matthew 5:16).

Who are the older people you remember with pleasure? I can think of so many who had some special quality about them that I'd like to incorporate into my own life. In this time of preparation for our senior years it would certainly be good to think about those older people we admire and stop to analyze just what it is that keeps them busy, cheerful and a source of inspiration to others.

I think of a white-haired lady I know who is reaching her middle 80's, but who is younger in heart than many women who have not lived half her number of years! She is the source of information about all those who are shut-in or hospitalized—and that information is not "second-hand" or hearsay—she has either made a personal visit or a personal phone call to find out for herself. If there is a time when the congregation comes together for any reason and she is not there, then she is checked on, for her absence is conspicuous. She is a wonderful correspondent—writing to all the missionaries of the church on a regular basis, as well as young people who are away in school or who are in military service. Her letters are cheerful, filled with everyday happenings (she keeps up with local ball games, etc.) and, of course, church news. I once told her that if I ever left our home town I would certainly deem it an honor to be on her mailing list. When my husband and I took a trip to Europe two years ago, guess whose letter was waiting for us when we arrived! You can see that as a result of this her mailbox is a means of travel and joy to her, and the letters are unselfishly shared with others of us who are either too lazy or uncaring perhaps to write. I could tell you many other things about her—she gets meals organized to take to the sick and bereaved; she shows her interest in both young and old by attending weddings and funerals; she actively participates in a garden club, etc. There are many things in her life worthy of setting up as a pattern.

Recently I attended the funeral of a very dear lady who had lived past the age of 103. Her life was one which had been spent in service to others just as long as she was able to serve as a practical nurse. Her town as well as her brothers and sisters in Christ honored her. Among the many nice compliments paid her in the funeral service was this one which seemed to sum up her life—"To be loved, you must love and be lovable." She was always pleasant to visit, never complaining or bemoaning her lot in life (although she lost her eyesight and was unable to walk the last few years of her life). Once I talked to her about a problem I had of waking up during the night, and she told me that when this happened to her she just lay still and repeated to herself scripture that she had earlier memorized. She was proud of the fact that she could remember over a hundred verses. Although she enjoyed living, I know that she had a faith built upon the belief that "the best is yet to be."

There are so many different ways in which we can prepare ourselves to enjoy the life promised for God's faithful children; but if we do not enjoy the time of preparation itself, then we had better reevaluate our training. If we are unproductive Christians, then we are miserable and unhappy. To the faithful Christian, service is a privilege instead of a burden. To see how you are actually growing, list the various areas in which you are active in the Lord's work. Take time to write them down and honestly judge yourself to see how much or how little you are doing. If your list is short, then remember that the abundant life is only for the productive.

Each new year my husband and I make a list of projects which we hope to accomplish during that current year. The list is always too long, and we find that we have to "roll some things forward" and try again the next year but it seems that an inventory of hopes, plans and abilities enables us to see more clearly and plan more productively than just letting things happen. Each one of us would make up a different list because we all differ, but standards are important and we owe it to God and to ourselves to make the most of our lives. It would be good to have a set of rules to check yourself against *daily*, much like the Boy Scouts do. Start off small and keep adding to it as your list becomes a habit.

1. Read and study my Bible.
2. Pray.
3. Visit someone outside my own family who needs encouragement—either by person, phone or mail.

As older Christian women we should be teaching the younger women by setting the best possible example (Titus 2:3-5). "Let the older women teach the younger" can apply to many. Teenage girls are able to help train younger girls; young married women can advise teenagers; middle-aged women can teach the young married, and so on. The scripture does not restrict the teaching from old to young but from old*er* to young*er*. In many cases there are younger who can teach the older, too. Let's not close our ears or eyes to examples of hospitality, eagerness to learn more about God's will and their willingness to talk to others about Christ. So many young women I know are learning to put first things first.

Jack Benny said, "Age is a matter of mind, and if you don't mind—it doesn't matter." To fight against growing old is to fight against God's law of life. We are all growing older each day we live, and it is impossible to stop the clock as it pertains to years. Although we cannot stay young, we can stay youthful! We do not need to be overly concerned about what we have to wear, what we have to eat, or other things of this nature. Worry is one of the best ways to put you in ill health, and we are not promised that illness and affliction will not affect the children of God. When I was young we lived next door to one of the most cheerful women I have ever known. She was a ray of sunshine to everyone who knew her. I remember that she used to say, "I have never been to the funeral of a Christian who starved to death!" I did not realize until later years just how sound that statement was—but think about it. Any faithful Christian who does his or her best to live a life of service is going to reap what he sows. If you do not visit, do not expect to be visited; if you do not show concern for others, then how can you truthfully find fault with those who are not concerned about you?

Whether you are a housewife or a business executive, retirement can be a breeze, depending upon your attitude toward it. I know that a housewife never reaches retirement in the same sense that a salaried person does, but when her children have established their own homes she naturally has fewer chores than she once did. A successful adjustment is the result of pre-retirement planning, and I believe more and more we are seeing the benefits from this. I recently read of a home economics teacher who was requiring her students to learn to knit, crochet and tat. She told them it was "rocking chair insurance." The day might come when they would live with their sons, and they needed to know how to keep busy with their hands so they would keep their fingers out of the daughter-in-law's hair. This is good advice for any reason. We all need to know how to keep busy in our old age to keep from being busy-bodies!

Retirement can be a happy time for those who keep active—physically, mentally and spiritually. For those who have taken care of their bodies there are physical sports in which they can continue. I know of a man who held a regular job as a bookkeeper, kept some individual sets of books at home, taught bowling twice a week and continued to win trophies himself until his 90's. Tennis, swimming, hiking, bicycling—all are enjoyed by people up in years. An active mind does not go stale. Keep up with what is going on in world affairs, read worthwhile books in addition to your Bible. In our church building we have a wonderful library but, sad to say, the habit of reading has not taken hold. Records and cassette tapes of sermons, hymns and inspirational talks are available, all of which can be listened to while you are ironing, cooking or cleaning house. If we feed our minds with spiritual food, then spiritual growth will surely follow and life becomes more meaningful each day we live!

Promises, promises, promises—the Bible is filled with them from beginning to end. We have been told in 2 Peter 3:9 that "the Lord is not slack concerning His promise." Sometimes, depending on our relationship with God, we could wish that He was. On the other hand, when we think about His promise to all who accept and obey His commandments, we know that our belief in the "best is yet to be" is a dream beyond our comprehension—a reason for our hope and perseverance throughout our earthly life. We sing so many songs descriptive of heaven, that wonderful place awaiting the faithful. One of the most descriptive says that "God shall wipe away all tears." Say the words aloud and you can understand why Paul said that to depart and be with Christ was far better than anything earth could offer.

Each day let us thank God for having let us live to that moment of time and each day determine that the best *is* yet to be.

Mrs. Honey McMacken
123 Treemont Drive
Tuscumbia, Alabama

BITS AND PIECES

Women sometimes enjoy reading sad tales of fact or fiction and having a good cry. Other times we prefer light, joyful reading. I hope this book has provided something for your every mood. Now, in this particular section (It could hardly be called a chapter, or even a lesson) I have attempted to combine a hundred or so unrelated subjects and to bind them together by bits and pieces. Among these souveniers and memories you will find everything from my own experiences growing up in the final years of the Depression to devotionals suitable for club meetings to modern proverbs and even favorite recipes collected over the years.

****

A fanatic is one who can't change her mind and won't change the subject.

****

PATIENCE is an attribute that most of us wish for more of. It is a child on the floor of the kitchen watching an ant carry its tremendous load (a dead fly) across the floor to the other side of the room and up the wall to the window only to find its load too big to go through the small opening of the screen wire. The child tries to help it by making the hole larger with an ice pick but the ant will not accept help. It goes through the hole alone. The child then takes the fly to the outside and lays it in front of the ant's path so that it will be sure to pick it up again. Perhaps this time it was grateful for the tiny creature again burdens itself with the big load and travels on. The ant's scrounging for food provides at least two hours of silent patience for the child, for he sits very still through the complete ordeal and sees the fly safely deposited into the ant's hill.

We usually think of children and patience synonymously. They just seem to go together. Every day of my life, I understand more fully the suggestion that God makes to adults that if we would enter heaven, we must first become as little children (Matthew 18:3). Patience is one attribute we sometimes lose as we grow up.

****

The most valuable gift you can give another is a good example.

****

Did you know that most people do not know what success is? I would venture to say that the majority think of succes in terms of $$$$ signs. Nowhere in the Bible do we read that to be successful we must have lots of money. This is human thinking; however, God's meaning of success is the attainment of peace of mind. It is also the realization of a situation or ideal—what the person is working toward. A person who is at peace with himself and with God is successful whether we think so or not.

And—did you know that most people follow the majority? The truth of the matter is that if we did the opposite of whatever the majority is doing we would probably come out much better. We should ask ourselves if the people we are following are going where we want to go. Most people take their first job simply on the recommendation of someone else.

Speaking of following the majority, what do most people do in their free time—NOTHING! Many of us watch TV every night. Why? Because of the total lack of decision. We do this because we follow what *most people* do, and *most people* have never learned how to live. We would be wise if we, before following *most people*, would ask ourselves what their goal in life is. What is the general attitude of the people I am following? Attitude is just about the most important word in the English language. People will react to us acording to our attitude. Are the people I am following "Thinking People?" The highest function of man is his ability to think. Everything else that man does can be done by every other animal. We can become whatever we imagine ourselves to be. If we are willing to simply follow the crowd, we will only end up wishing to repeat the whole situation. So far as we know, we can't. Be careful what you think about; this is what you will become. If we develop a positive mental attitude we can reach any goal.

****

A company is known by the men it keeps.

****

One day while buying groceries, I had just gotten started and was already befuddled with decisions concerning the coming week's menus—wishing for that 1002nd way to disguise hamburger meat, wondering what we would have for supper that very night and hoping the budget would stretch far enough. Right in front of me I noticed a most delightful woman who through conversation I learned was a missionary wife from the Bermuda Islands. When I heaved a great sigh in her presence and uttered a discouraging word and hungry groan, she said, "Let me tell you something that is delicious, easy to fix and inexpensive." Well, I assure you that combination is hard to beat! So here is the recipe she gave me, which we have enjoyed more than any other recipe we have ever tried. As I pass it on to you, I ask you then to pass it on to others. This act will always be your good deed for the day if you have no other.

Corned Beef and Cabbage and Other Good Things

Place all ingredients in a large dutch oven in this order. Cook on medium heat until it starts boiling (or sometimes for me, burning) then turn it down to low. Let it simmer until done (about 2 hours).

1. Melt ½ stick margarine in big skillet or dutch oven (one with a cover).
2. Wash and cut up a cabbage head in the melted oleo. The size of the cabbage will depend on the size of your family.
3. Cut up as many carrots on top of the cabbage as you need for your family.
4. Cut up a large onion over the carrots.
5. Next comes potatoes—as many as you need. Peel and quarter them over the onion.
6. Last, open one or two cans of corned beef and fork it out of the can and over the potatoes. Sprinkle the whole thing with salt and pepper, put the lid on and turn the eye down to simmer. Let it cook until the vegetables are tender, especially the carrots.

With a dish like this and a skillet of cornbread, who could want more?

****

There are few, if any jobs in which ability alone is sufficient. Needed also are loyalty, sincerity, enthusiasm and cooperation.

****

God led the children of Israel with a pillar of fire by night and a cloud by day. He leads us with glorious promises. We live each day renewed by His promises and do our best to fulfill the responsibility that measures us up to that reward. We must be ever ready for the opportunities sure to come our way. We must never give way to self-pity or defeat.

I read just the other day of an account which proved to me very vividly the fact that we never use all of our ability and the fact that we can do anything we determine to do. It seems that a little girl visiting her grandmother was told by her grandmother about a certain rock down several hundred feet from the house on the bank of a little creek. She wanted the rock moved from its place on the creek to the side of the back porch near the steps. The little girl made many trips to look at the rock but came back to the grandmother reporting that it was impossible for her, a little seven-year-old girl, to even move the rock much less bring it to the house. Each time the grandmother would tell her she could and must bring the rock to the house. Finally she told her to try only to move it inch by inch if that was the only way she could maneuver it. After many days the big rock was finally scooted, dragged, rolled and pushed to the side of the porch near the back steps. With a tremendous let-go sigh, the little girl said, "Grandmother, the rock is here where you wanted it. Now what do you intend to do with it?" "Oh, not a thing dear," the grandmother said, "I don't even want the rock, but I had you to move it so as to teach you a lesson that you must never forget as long as you live. By moving that huge impossible rock you proved that you can do anything you set out to do if you want to do that thing strongly enough." And so it is!

****

"I can do all things through Christ which strengtheneth me" (Philippians 4:13).

****

The person who gets ahead is the one who does more than is necessary and keeps on doing it.

****

Concerning certain simple matters we sometimes *know* we are right, and there is no question about it! Then it is a real blow to our ego to have to find out and even admit we are wrong in our thinking.

Consider, for example, my ideas concerning religion and politics when I was growing up. Mama was a very strong Christian and Papa was a very strong Republican. I am being very honest when I tell you that I grew up thinking that everybody who was a Christian was also a Republican. It was a real shock to me to find out differently—that some Christians were also Democrats and vice versa.

You may chuckle at my ignorance, but isn't this the way our faith comes about many times? We embrace whatever our parents believed, right or wrong. Millions of people are going to find themselves in the same predicament at the judgment—telling God our Father, who created us and the universe, that He is wrong and that our salvation can't possibly hinge on those simple statements in the Bible. Mama, Papa, preacher, priest or someone else told us another way. And they can't be wrong! It doesn't change our destiny one bit if we cling to the beliefs of our fathers and forefathers if what they believed is wrong. We are responsible for our own salvation. We must make our calling and election sure (2 Peter 1:10).

****

If you tell a man there are 300 billion stars in the universe, he'll believe you; but if you tell him a bench has just been painted, he has to touch it to be sure.

****

If you want to eat the very best potato—ever—try this!

Parmesan Potatoes

(You can also shake your cut-up chicken pieces in this same coating mixture and bake in the same dish.)

6 large potatoes (about 3 lbs.)
¼ c. sifted flour
¼ c. grated parmesan cheese
¾ tsp. salt

1/8 tsp. pepper
⅓ c. butter
chopped parsley

Pare potatoes; cut into quarters. Combine flour, cheese, salt and pepper in a bag. Moisten potatoes with water and shake a few at a time in a bag, coating potatoes well with cheese mixture. Melt butter in a 13" x 9" baking pan or dish. Place potatoes in a layer in pan. Bake at 375 degrees for about 1 hour, turning once during baking. When golden brown, sprinkle with parsley. Makes 6 to 8 servings. Scrumptuous!

****

The secret word is—help. Just plain help. Not, help? Or H E L P ! Just help. Like kindness or compassion, help is needed by every living person. No one is an island. Everyone needs help in one way or another—rich, poor, male, female.

Jesus helped more people in His three short ministering years than, if put in books, the world could contain. When an opportunity comes for us to be of help, we are sometimes tempted to call Mrs. Soandso on the benevolent committee at church or this source or that foundation. We ought always to accept every challenge and stop belittling ourselves. *We can help* or we wouldn't have been called on in the first place. *I can help.* We need only to look to the hills from whence cometh our help and pass it on. It is a warm feeling to know we are needed. It is comforting and rewarding to help someone and know they've been helped. Let this be a day of helpfulness; be on the lookout for other's needs.

****

A leader has two important characteristics: first, he is going somewhere; second, he is able to persuade other people to go with him.

****

Burdens. Do we sometimes let our responsibilities become burdens? Who is to say their burden is heavier? If our back becomes weary and our shoulders heavy, then it becomes a comfort to read and picture Jesus bidding us come and rest and take off the heavy pack from our shoulders and let Him carry it for us. You remember He said, "Come to me, all of you who are weary and are over-burdened, and I will give you rest!

Put on my yoke and learn from me. For I am gentle and humble in heart and you will find rest for your souls. For my yoke is easy and my burden is light'' (Matthew 11:28-30 Phillips).

If you knew you were about to be killed for being a Christian, would you feel that your burden was light? I hardly see how you could. Only our Lord and Savior could say this. We all complain and carry on sometimes about our crosses and tell others our troubles. While they listen, they are thinking how small ours are in comparison to theirs. If we could only learn to remain cheerful, though burdened, we would come through triumphant. Burdens are a part of our discipline. Don't falter under the weight of a burden. Learn to smile and pray and share. Share your burden. Jesus will help carry it and so will your friends.

****

A man rarely succeeds at anything unless he has fun doing it.

****

People can be divided into three groups: those who make things happen, those who watch things happen, and those who wonder what happened.

****

Discouragement. Is that a Christian word? Surely not. But then, maybe it is. Christians, as well as those of the world, certainly dispense it often enough and take it on as a cloak on a wintry day. We become chilled through and through with it and never seem to realize that warmth is waiting in the form of faith if we will only seek it.

My first effort toward getting something published would never have gone beyond my mailbox if I had been willing to become discouraged. This discouragement did not come from the world, either; it came from my brothers and sisters in Christ. Some would ask me if I knew how very difficult it is these days to get something published (which I didn't). Did I know what the cost would be? (I didn't.) Was I a professional writer? (I'm not a professional anything.) Did I honestly believe a busy publisher would read my manuscript? (Maybe I would catch him on one of his less busy days.)

These are only a few of the discouragements thrown my way. Then a cause of despair came from one whom I loved and respected very, very much. He read what we had written and then said, "Take my advice and just don't try to get this published; then you won't be disappointed." But there were a few things that these "helpful" people hadn't counted on! When someone tells me a thing can't be done, it makes me just 10 times as determined to show them that it can. God told us that nothing was impossible. Whatever man imagines himself to do, he can do (Genesis 11:6). "I can do all things through Christ which strengtheneth me" (Philippians 4:13). If we, as Christians, don't believe this we might just as well do what most people do—NOTHING!

I should go on and tell you that our book, *What are We Doing Here?*, was published and sold and sold and sold. It is still (at this writing) selling well. The profits are given to Mars Hill Bible School. My advice: if someone discourages you in a new venture (and I can assure you they will), take it with a positive attitude and show them that they are wrong. You and God can accomplish any impossible task!

****

The goal of criticism is to leave the person with the feeling he has been helped.

****

How to Win Friends and Influence People! No, I'm not about to infringe on Dale Carnegie's knowledge. How to win friends and influence people is what I call this most delicious cake. Every time I pass it on to a friend, the before-mentioned title is what I tell her to call it. Later on, I always hear, "You know, it works! I served that cake to friends, and they went on and on about it, always exclaiming over one more slice of cake, until it is gone."

Whether you make your layers from scratch or from a mix doesn't really matter. Just make two layers of white cake, let them cool, then split them making four layers. Frost them with this marvelous frosting:

1 carton (½ pint) sour cream
2 cups powdered sugar
3 cups frozen coconut or fresh grated coconut (not canned)

Stir sour cream and sugar until well mixed, then add coconut. Mix well, put frosting between all four layers. Now here is a scrumptious variation:

2 cups powdered sugar
1 carton sour cream
1½ cups grated coconut
1½ cups drained, crushed pineapple

Follow above instructions. Out of this world!

****

There are many good Bible translations today but the best translation of the Bible to be found anywhere is the one lived in the lives of true Christians, for this is the only version that the majority of people ever read.

****

FAITH is another virtue that all children possess. It, too, is destroyed during our growing up years if we are not ever so careful. The youth of today blame their lack of faith on their parents. They say we have double standards, and I am sure this is true many times. I don't appreciate double standards any more than the most rebellious young man or woman does. Watching while others say to do this and do that while they, themselves, do the opposite can trigger a hatred button in us and cause us to dump every worthwhile virtue we possess in one big heap and start us miserably down hill, hating everything in our path. We do not impress or influence anyone with hatred. It shortens our life span and costs us our place in heaven. We can learn so much from children. They have perfect faith and complete confidence in those they love. Their trust and faith is so natural and has such simplicity. It is our influence and ugliness that mars a child's trust. While we are supplied daily lessons in love, trust, patience and faith from children, let us strive to make ourselves worthy of their trust. Children imitate as they grow. They learn how to deceive and hate from us. Hate and deception have to be taught. Careless words and devilish deeds sewn before a child take root and grow, not of themselves but with our help. We heap on more of the same, day by day, and the first thing we know, we have a rebellious young man or woman on our hands, screaming back into our ears. We have reaped our harvest. 16 or 17 years of cultivating a tender mind reaps either wheat or tares.

****

It is a common thing now for "R" rated movies to be on prime-time TV. The other day one such movie was being discussed which was to be shown that night. The mother talking told the youngest of her children that he would have to go to his room while that particular movie was on. He said, "Are you going to watch it, Mother?" Her reply was, "Yes, but you can't." He said, "If it's alright for mothers, why isn't it alright for little boys?" I believe we should think about that. If a movie or any other show on TV is obscene, is it really fit for any member of the family to watch? I believe this is another of our double standards.

****

GOODNESS. Do you know that the only way we can show others that we are good is by our deeds? We could tell everyone in town that we are good and it would mean nothing, absolutely nothing, to them. Only when they see our works would anyone know that we are good. There must be proof. Of what use is the fruit tree that never blooms or bears fruit? Even the grandest oak tree standing bears acorns. They are dropped round about to show us its works. When a hungry child comes to your door, a kind word helps but does not fill his stomach. Two little beggar boys have stopped by our house twice a day since they were big enough to walk. They are now 12 or 13 years old and still stopping twice every day. Many times I sinned by telling them to go on—I had nothing for them. I would always repent and give them twice as much the next time. One day one of the little boys said, "Woman," (they never learned to call me by my name) "your house is on our way to *everywhere*." "God loveth a cheerful giver" (2 Corinthians 9:7). This trait has not always been true nor easy for me, but I'm working on it.

****

Men do not stumble over mountains, but over molehills.

****

A little girl in one of our Bible school classes was asked by her teacher how old she was. "I'm 4," said Jamie. "When will you be 5?" asked her teacher. "When I get to my thumb," Jamie said most assuredly.

****

Temper is what gets most of us in trouble. Pride keeps us there.

****

It takes less time to do a thing right than to explain why you did it wrong.

****

You never get a second chance to make a good first impression.

****

The seven stages of ambition: to be like dad; to be an engineer; to pilot an airplane; to be famous; to become a millionaire; to make both ends meet; to hang on long enough to draw a pension.

****

Patrick Henry said, "Give me liberty or give me death." His successor of a future generation shouted, "Give me liberty." Unfortunately, the men of our generation have shortened all this to two words, "Give me."

****

Men solve complicated problems better than women, it is said. But did a man ever keep the faces of three chocolate-eating kids clean with a six-inch handkerchief?

****

To a child thrust into a strange world, a good teacher is the best thing that can possibly happen.

A teacher is Courage with facial tissues in its pocket, Sympathy struggling with a snowsuit and Patience with papers to grade.

Teachers spend 12 hours a day searching for truth and the other 12 hours searching for error. They are indispensable, invincible and nearly inexhaustible.

A teacher really does not mind sniffles, squirmings, stomachaches, spills, sloth and sauciness. Neither does she disintegrate before tears, trifles, fights, futility, excuses, parents who spout, little boys who shout and little girls who pout.

Most of all, a teacher is someone who likes someone else's children—and still has enough strength left to go to the P.T.A. meeting. Thank heaven for good teachers.

****

Seven Stages of Woman:
In her infancy she needs love and care . . . In her childhood she wants fun . . . In her teen years she wants excitement . . . In her twenties she wants romance . . . In her thirties she wants admiration . . . In her forties she wants sympathy . . . In her fifties she wants cash.

****

We learn from experience. A man never wakes up his second baby just to see him smile.

****

What we do for ourselves alone dies with us; what we do for others remains and is immortal.

****

In our Bible school class we were beginning a study of foreign mission work and the evangelists. We had prepared a letter for the children to sign and add a line if they wished. We had planned to seal and mail them, a copy to each of 11 families whom our congregation supports, when we decided that maybe we should look over what the children had written. One little boy ended his note with, "Thank you and we are *paying* for you."

****

A little girl in our Bible class was so excited over a party dress her mother was making for her. It was for a very special occasion. The mother was sewing little pearls and sequins down the front. The little girl remarked to me very excitedly that her new dress had "secrets" sewed on it.

Thinking about this later brought to mind just how easily we can misinterpret words and think they mean one thing when they have an entirely different meaning. The Bible tells us to study for ourselves. Look up words. Be curious. Wonder about things. Answers make us wise; questions make us human.

****

We have more today than at any other time in history; yet more people are trying to escape by taking tranquilizers. Why? I believe it is because people outside of Christ search just the same as people inside. If a world and its wealth could make us a happy people, then King Solomon would have known complete bliss. This was not the case, though, and is not the answer today. Something to live with and die for—something to die for and live with: this is happiness.

Glenda Reid
Cherokee, Alabama

****

FOR MOTHERS ONLY

Over and over I said the word, Under my breath, yet I hoped she heard:
"Sorry," I said in my mother's direction, In the next room, she was sewing
Protection,
Against the winter for eight little girls . . . How gently, how easily, memory
unfurls,
Showing my mother's slow widening smile, "I knew you were sorry all the
while,"
She said as she kissed me and dried my tears, And I kept thinking what
wonderful ears,
My mother must have to hear what I say, Under my breath and a room away.

****

The only thing that gives you more for your money than it did ten years ago is the penny when you weigh yourself at the corner drugstore.

****

Many tasks seem simple to one who has not tried to perform them.

****

Of all the things you wear, your expression is the most important.

****

The great dividing line between success and failure can be expressed in five words: "I did not have time."

****

Postscripts from Peg on Hospitality: Ten tips for young mothers from a used one:

1. Do keep in touch with your friends by having meals together that are the least amount of work—hamburgers, potato chips and cokes and/or tea, for example. Serve make-ahead dishes such as spaghetti that require no or maybe only one side dish. (Sauce can be made ahead and so can slaw.) Don't mind repeating the same menu if it is something you really enjoy.

2. Do try to make your house childproof. I believe it is a mistake to leave breakables down for 2-year-olds to reach. If they are put away for the time, say until he reaches age 4, he can then understand what you say to him, and mother's nerves have been preserved. Don't try to spank infants into leaving things alone. They do not and cannot understand. If there is any way possible for you to arrange to have your second baby first, this is the thing to do. By the time the second child comes along you have a much more relaxed attitude.

3. If you have guests with small children, here are some suggestions for their entertainment and your own children as well: set of sponges and aluminum pie pans, Daddy's plastic fishing worms, teakettles and old lampshades, old purses filled with plastic jewelry, empty lipstick tubes (well cleaned), old powder puffs and a small comb.

4. Do find the time to read—the daily newspaper, good novels, news magazines, etc—so that you can keep up with what is going on in the world. The conversation will be much more interesting if you have something to talk about other than the children. Husbands like to be able to talk occasionally, and it is good to be informed on subjects of interest to him.

5. Don't ever mind spending money for babysitters. The best medicine in the world for the "housewife blues" is to call a sitter and plan a date

with your husband. There is nothing noble in the statement "We don't leave our children with sitters." A prominent doctor gave me this advice when our children were small, and I have found it to be true: "Don't call on relatives or your best friends to babysit for you. You do not relax while you are away for fear the children are misbehaving. Hire someone dependable, then go out and relax without feeling guilty."

6. Write notes. When you are tied down with little ones, there is not much time left to do anything outside the home such as visiting or any sort of personal work. You can write notes. It is a wonderful habit to form. Send notes to the sick, bereaved and those celebrating birthdays (especially senior citizens).

7. Several times a year in our area special children's concerts are scheduled at the fine arts center. It is good to take children to these concerts and expose them to good music, drama and other fine arts. Form car pools and go to these concerts. You'll be glad you did.

8. Learn to be a good listener. We all know people who take up all your time telling their own tales of woe. They do not take turns and listen to you. Listening is an art. I have a friend who really listens to every word being said and is not thinking of interrupting with a word of her own. She is loved by everyone who knows her, for she makes you feel as if what you are saying is the most important thing she has ever heard.

9. Learn to keep a confidence. This virtue is priceless. I once knew a girl who went to a church leader for counseling in a matter of importance. The elder went to parties outside those involved and discussed the problem and caused much strife. Leave other people's business with other people. Take only that which is given to you in confidence and keep it. Guard it with your heart. God will bless you for it.

10. "Confess your faults one to another." I know, truly, that one of the main reasons God told us to do this is so that we can improve ourselves. The simple matter of saying, "Thank you," is sometimes so very difficult to say. For me this has always been a problem. When someone says to me "That's a pretty dress," what do you think I say? Not a simple, "Thank you." I usually say, "Oh, it's old," or "I've never liked it much." It is as if that person said, "Is that a new dress you're wearing?" or "Do you like the dress you're wearing?"

****

My friend, speak always once,
but listen twice . . . .
This , I would have you know
is sound advice;
For God hath given you
and all your peers
A single mouth, old friend,
but a pair of ears.

****

Don't look back. Isn't it true that if you try to walk forward with your head turned to face what's behind, you will stumble? Paul did not tell us to press ever forward for no reason. Neither was the lesson of Lot's wife recorded just to take up space. Usually in reading magazines, newsletters or bulletins you will notice about as many fillers as there are worthwhile articles. God's book is not like that. He has no fillers. Mrs. Lot was told, as was the rest of her family, not to look back. What do you suppose is the most logical explanation for this?

The other day I heard of a woman who was so distressed and emotionally sick that she was near a mental collapse. She called her minister to her house, confessed her sin and asked him to pray for her. "I cannot do that," he said.

His statement shocked her back into reality long enough to ask why.

"Last year you called me to come to visit you. I came, and you confessed this very same sin at that time. We prayed together. God forgave you. Now, if we pray to God for forgiveness today for the same sin, He will not know what we are talking about."

That woman was still looking back and stumbling over obstacles that should not have been there. She had failed to forgive herself. This is the hardest thing in the world for many of us to do. We continue to feel guilty over something that took place five, 10 or 20 years ago, and that guilt feeling eats away at our conscience and nags us to the point of mental breakdown.

The answer, it seems to me, for this problem and just about every problem involving our minds is to get so involved in something worthwhile, particularly the Lord's work, that we don't have time to think of what we have left behind.

****

The past is a nice place to visit, but I wouldn't want to live there.

****

Eyes are where they are—for looking ahead.

****

A clock was placed in the new church building at the back of the auditorium with this sign under it: "Remember Lot's wife."

****

LIKE MOTHER LIKE SON

Do you know that your soul is of my soul such a part,
That you seem to be fibre and core of my heart?
None other can please me or praise me as you,
Remember the world will be quick with its blame.
If shadow or stain ever darken your name.
"Like mother, like son" is a saying so true,
The world will judge largely the "Mother" by you.
Be yours then the task, if task it shall be,
To force the proud world to do homage to me.
Be sure it will say, when its verdict you've won,
"She reaped as she sowed, Lo! This is her son."

****

I AM THANKFUL. . .for good health, and for the food that I have each day. I am thankful for those near and dear to me that I can love, and in turn love me. I am thankful for the freedom of my nation, and that I can worship without conflict. I am thankful that God loved me so much, that he provided a way for my salvation. I am thankful that he is a forgiving Father. I am thankful that I can attend the worship of my Lord with so many of my brothers and sisters.

****

Do you ever long for a taste of those good ole fried peach pies like Mama or Grandma used to make? With the price of dried fruit these days, those days may be gone forever. However, through the wisdom of a wonderful farm wife, here is a recipe for making fresh peaches suitable for fried pies. As a matter of fact, you cannot tell they are not dried peaches. I hope you will treasure this recipe as I do.

PEACHES FOR FRIED PIES

2 gallons unpeeled cut-up peaches
6-8 cups sugar
2 cups vinegar

Mix and cook until thick or until consistency of peach preserves (it should not be too runny or juicy). Put in hot pint jars while boiling hot and seal; or you can let cool and put in freezer containers and freeze. When you are ready to make pies, simply make your pastry and cut into 5'' circles. Fill one side of circle with peaches and dot with butter. Moisten edges of dough with water and fold other half of dough over peaches and seal edges of pie by pressing edge together with fork. This is one of my prize recipes.

****

During those worrisome times when your children get on your nerves and you feel like screaming—don't. Stop. Take a deep breath and treat them as if they belonged to someone else.

****

God has put a fence around sex—He calls it marriage.

****

Can you remember how excited you felt when you finally reached the dating age and *that boy* asked you for your first date? Remember the pride you felt when you graduated from high school or the thrill when you took the wheel of your first car? Your wedding day was such a special, beautiful event and then the glorious moment when you first held your baby in your arms. Surely these are some of the most important and memorable events in a girl's life. Then you see your own children begin to blossom and take hold of these same events in their own lives, and you begin to feel surely this is the most important part of a woman's life. However, none of these things can even approach what has to be the most important event in any person's life—obeying the Gospel! Obeying the Lord's command and dedicating one's life to Him and being baptized to seal the covenant between you and Him is certainly the most important event ever to take place on this wonderful earth that God has given us.

Living the Christian life is certainly not without its sorrows, but we know that the most compassionate person who ever lived is there at the right hand of God taking our side. When we've done wrong and have repented, He is there talking to God as our earthly big brother might sometimes take our side to our parents saying, "Father, don't be too harsh on her; she didn't mean any harm. Please, Father."

A Christian has something that no one else has—open communication with God through prayer and His Word. Only God's children have the privilege.

****

Be kind. Remember, everyone you meet is fighting a battle.

Mrs. Peggy Simpson
406 W. North Commons
Tuscumbia, Alabama